THE MARQUISE HILL STORY

THE MARQUISE HILL STORY

FROM THE CRADLE TO THE BOWL

SHERRY HILL

Library of Congress Control Number: 2008906363
ISBN: Hardcover 978-1-4363-5690-9
Softcover 978-1-4363-5689-3

This book was printed in the United States of America.

To order additional copies of this book, contact:
Xlibris Corporation
1-888-795-4274
www.Xlibris.com
Orders@Xlibris.com

50867

Contents

Dedication

To my baby boy, Marquise Yannick Hill, who passed away in May 2007, and to my oldest brother, James M. Hill, who passed away in November after Katrina. You have always been my heroes all the way.

Mrs. Virgie Chancellor, you placed that little sunshine in my son's life when he was growing up by creating the Sunshine Band. Coach Jeff Boss—may you rest in peace.

My late grandparents, Rev. Lafayette Bennett and Alberta Lee Bennett, and Mr. and Mrs. Lawson Hill and Bertha Porter Hill; *my aunt Mrs. Betsy L. Smith and my uncle, Rev. LeMickel Bennett.* You are missed.

Albert "Skinny" - Elias, Sr., who was a mentor to my son before his untimely passing after Katrina.

Acknowledgements

I would like to give thanks to God first and foremost; my mother, Elmira Bennett Hill, who has been there for me from day one; my father, Richard Hill; my stepmother, Virginia Hill; my brothers—Marcus, Aaron, and Daniel and their families, my grandson for being the precious boy he is, as well as all my other relatives and associates. More thanks go to my editor, Natalie G. Owens, as well as to my beloved friends, my coworkers at NFC and the New Orleans Police Department for supporting me throughout the difficult times.

I wish to also show my appreciation to my son's friend from middle school, Michael Boyd, who faces a battle with illness. Marquise never forgot Michael, whom he had watched taking care of his mother who subsequently died of the same condition. Marquise wanted to do something special for Michael before his untimely death, but unfortunately, he lost his life before he could. Michael attended the funeral in a wheelchair. Thank you for being special, Michael!

Last but not the least, I would like to thank the following wonderful people and organizations who have, in different ways, inspired my son and helped him fulfill his purpose and dreams and honored him after his passing:

Greater St. Stephen Church family
Bishop Paul S. Morton and Co-Pastor Deborah B. Morton
Mr. Robert Kraft, owner of the New England Patriots
Coach Bill Belicheck
The Patriot fans—every last one!
Marquise's NEP teammates—every last one!
The National Football League
LSU teammates and fans and the Athletic Department
Max Emfinger's Top 100 National Blue Chips
The Ohio Touchdown Club
Fox Sports, *Countdown to Signing Day*
DeLaSalle High School and staff

Ed Daniels, Channel 26 Sports News
Dennis Waltering, Channel 4
Louisiana Weekly
New Orleans Police Department
National Finance Center
Rivals.com
Sports Illustrated
Amani Martin, HBO, *Inside the NFL*
NFL Network
Karen Crouse, *NY Times*
Dennis Hodges, for the LSU photos
Tiger Rags
Purple and Gold
Louisiana Football Magazine
ESPN *Prep Football* magazine and show
Gloria Johnson, Orleans Parish School
Tom Lemming
Dandy Don
Times-Picayune
USA Today All-American Team Selection Committee
Boston Herald
Nancy Lane
John Wilcox
Bob Hohler, *Boston Globe*
Pastor Johnny Harris
Nancy Lane
John Tomase
Laurel J. Sweet
Denicola Furniture Concepts
Mr. Edward Wells, eighth-grade teacher at Fannie C. Williams New Orleans Middle School.
Mrs. Odea Bowman Assistand principal at Fannie C. William Middle School Orleans Parish School
Orleans Parish School Board
Mr. and Mrs. Gelpi
Baton Rouge Advocate newspaper
SuperPrep magazine
Toastmasters International
Jacob Schoen Funeral Home
Allen Temple COGIC

Mckernan Law Firm, Baton Rouge
Josh Eagerman, Standard Times
Jeff Majors, TV ONE
Chicago Times
Pearlie Elloie, Director of Head Start
Edward Lewis, *Louisiana Weekly*
The Jet Magazine
ACA Archdioceses Witness Program (New Orleans Summer Program)
James Rambeau Esq.
Coach G Matthews DLS coach
Darren Barbier DLS coach
Mr. & Mrs. Reynold Ralph
Sam Nader LSU
Lake Pontchartrain: Volunteer Rescue Workers and Coast Guard
Dr Emile LeBranche III MD
Coach Pete Jenkins
Dr Linda D White MD
Scott Mckay and David Whitmore
Kevin Blakes
All Marquise's Fans—every last one!

In Memory of Marquise Hill

"The recently established New England Patriots Locker Room in memory of Marquise Y. Hill. My thanks, and those of my family, are extended to the Patriots Organization for this kind gesture."

Author's Message for Parents

It is my viewpoint that one should discuss important family matters with one's children and, therefore, never leave them out of the process when it comes to dealing with events that affect the whole family. I would make sure that Marquise never forgot that his mother was there to support him and defend his interests in everything that he did, leaving the door open all times, both as a parent and as a best friend.

It is important to keep in mind never to talk down to our children or to fill their heads with negative ideas about themselves or someone else, such as criticizing them or even another parent or relative. A parent needs to watch what he or she says because words can have a huge impact on a child's self-esteem. Take note that your children are watching you in the same way you are always watching them. We must also remember that children are our future, and it is our responsibility to mold them into healthy human beings and to provide them with the requisite skills to cope with life and face challenges, whenever they present themselves, with courage and determination.

Sometimes a parent's job is hard to do. So a parent should seek help when needed, especially when they are dealing with so many major issues that influence our children today, such as negative habits, drugs, gangs, etc. This type of behavior will have an impact on your child. Denial, however, is the worse solution to this recurring problem of the modern world. When you deny something so vital and so obvious, everyone knows that you have a problem but you, and it doesn't make you look responsible at all. A child can respect you so much more if you admit to a problem rather than refuse to accept its existence. If you don't acknowledge such a fact, you will be surprised how it will come back to haunt you later in life. Make sure that, as a parent, you are in order—your child will pick up on it in some way or another. How is a child to learn good habits if his or her parents cannot adopt those habits themselves? Children learn from example, and trust me, they never stop watching you.

My son was no different. He told me so many times, years ago, "Ma, I have watched you struggle to provide for me throughout the years and never once did I hear you complain about it. The only times you were upset is when I did not do something that you asked of me. I also saw many of my friends and classmates who grew up with both their mother and father, but they still had problems as well. I have talked to many of my friends whose parents' marriage was on the rocks, and they did not know which way to go. I had other friends who had everything they could ever want, except love, and still they were not happy. After seeing all this, I have learned to appreciate what I had at home growing up."

My son was wise beyond his years. From the mind of a young man barely turned twenty, these words seem almost out of place—these lessons in life are normally learned at a more mature age. But in my eyes, Marquise was extraordinary—as every son is in every mother's eyes and, thus, in her heart. I hope that this book will give you a little glimpse into the type of person my son was, and I also hope that you will be able to see yourself in some ways through his journey, his energy, and his challenges.

Introduction

My son had a heart of gold. He loved to see peoples' faces brighten with a smile, especially children and youth. Perhaps it is because of the way I raised him to be conscious of others. After all, it is the way I was also raised. Despite the myriad problems that plagued my family during my childhood and youth, both my parents taught me and my brothers to have a heart and to always care for the poor and unfortunate.

I will never forget when my mother brought an elderly woman in our home in the late 1970s. She had been living in her home, destitute and sitting in her own excrement. Somehow, she had fallen in the fireplace, and her arm was burned to the bone. The woman had not received a doctor's care for about a year, and she was in such a state that she couldn't remember when the incident had happened.

My mother took her first to the hospital for care and then to our house. She bathed the woman, cut her hair, and groomed her. The older woman was so thankful that she couldn't help crying. From that episode, I learned to appreciate the kindness of my parents and the importance of compassion. My mother would say, "I would have missed my blessing if I left the lady in those conditions." She told my father that there was no way she would allow the lady to go back and live in that same, neglected way. My father supported her decision. Later, the old lady lost her memory, and she began to wander. Scared that she'd hurt herself, my mother was forced to place her in a home so she could get round-the-clock care. When she died, my parents made sure she received a proper burial. Her daughter had passed away years earlier, leaving a mentally challenged son behind, so it was up to us to take responsibility for things.

My son knew the story, and both my mother and I made sure he grew up to *care* for others. To continue his legacy, I will be instituting and running a nonprofit in his name: the Marquise Hill Foundation. The purpose of the foundation will be to help disadvantaged youth of all races and beliefs. I will be infinitely proud to do this work on Marquise's behalf.

It is my hope that with this book, I am able to introduce readers to my son, Marquise Hill, a born athlete and an incredible human being, who tragically passed away in May 2007. I would like everybody to feel as if they had known him in his lifetime, in a way as familiar and beloved as a well-worn, comfortable house shoe.

My son was a great young man and a talented athlete who grew up way too fast and took his responsibilities seriously. You will witness his transition from a baby to a toddler, from a little boy to a young man, and finally to a responsible adult. By the age of twenty-four, he had achieved many things the average person would only dream about. He went from being the product of a modest household to achieving success in the Sugar Bowl with the LSU Tigers and, ultimately, to fulfilling his dream of taking his team, the New England Patriots, to the ultimate glory of the Super Bowl.

He did it all through God-given talent, lots of love, sheer hard work, drive, optimism, and strength of will. However, my intention is not to give you his sports stats—you can find those on any website on the Internet or various sports magazines. I will, of course, delve somewhat into his athletic career. But this book will give you above all else the human face of Marquise Hill.

I want to present to you my Marquise, the man, the person he was, before I describe the athlete he became. He was primarily a man who helped and inspired others the way he was helped and inspired in life. A man who faced challenges with a strong heart and unparalleled determination. A man who cherished life and saw the humor and philosophy in all things. He was truly an individual wise beyond his years, and I say this not because he was my son, but because it was just so.

My son's life story is worth telling. Marquise and I had started talking about writing his life story a long time ago. It is undoubtedly ironic that I finally decided to start writing on a Thursday, exactly four days before his tragic accident wrought by the vicious currents in Lake Pontchartrain.

I hope that through these pages onto which I have unreservedly poured my heart and soul, you will come to love Marquise, if not in the way I loved him as a mother and friend, at least in the way you would treasure a trusted, well-missed, departed friend.

***NOTE*:** The names of certain people mentioned in this book have been changed to protect their privacy. Janice Meeks and Darrell Jackson are fictitious names for real people.

I

BEFORE THE DAY HE WAS BORN

Before I jump into writing about my son, I would first like to give you, dear reader, a little insight into my background and circumstances. I believe that knowing to some degree where I came from will give you a better understanding as to why I lived the life I lived and why I made the decisions I made when it came to caring for my greatest treasure, my son, Marquise. So for your benefit, let me tell you how it all started . . .

Early one morning, when I was approximately four months pregnant, I was walking to the bus stop and Marquise was flipping in my stomach. It felt like he was already telling me that he wanted to play football and that it would be his destiny. I was walking and crying on this crisp March New Orleans morning because, just a few weeks earlier, Marquise's father had turned his back to me and walked away from our relationship, telling me he could not, and would not, provide support for this baby he helped conceive. Deceitfulness had invaded my life through this man, who I had earlier regarded as a friend. When I met Marquise's father, I was at a time in my life when I needed friendship and support more so than a relationship; but he let me down on all fronts, playing games I wasn't ready to deal with. When I told him about the pregnancy, he suggested I had other options available to me if I didn't want to become a mother and he said I knew what I had to do.

I cried because of the fact that I myself was the product of a broken home. In fact, I had previously—way before I met my son's father in New Orleans, way back when I lived in Alabama—moved away from a terrible home environment (this was way before I got pregnant) because of that very reason. I had never been a problem child to my parents. I struggled through college, but did graduate in 1979, always trying to be a good girl with worthy aspirations. I wanted to earn a good education and become a renowned artist. I have been gifted with a talent and love for painting portraits. I wanted to nourish that talent that God gave me.

However, things are not always what they seem, and my family suffered the same fate in unraveling as so many others do in our society. Unfortunately, the pressure of so much distraction and temptation is hard to bear by many, and my world was no exception. Now, in my mind, as I found myself pregnant and jilted, history was repeating itself in the most miserable of ways. At a young age, most problems seem so much larger, so much more definite and final, so much more devastating.

Devastating, just like the time I was almost raped, at the age of fourteen, back in Alabama. For a long time, I was afraid of men and relationships. It took me a while to tell my parents about it. It was a dark secret that made me feel vulnerable and scared. I became very cautious around others, but healing came after a while, thankfully, as it often does with time. I had the same aspirations that any young girl would have, and I was very resolved to succeed. I told my son about it when he grew up, and I think that knowing this about me and seeing my approach to life, he understood why I had such a strong will.

Notwithstanding or perhaps because of all of this, from the get-go, despite my artistic ambitions and the challenges I faced, I had simple dreams when it came down to my personal life—to meet the right man who would love and cherish me, have a perfect wedding, and raise my family in harmony. Everybody has these dreams, don't they? No matter what is one's status, personality, race, beliefs, or culture, these are dreams that bind many different people under these common desires. Some don't like to admit it, but few people would rather live their life alone forever.

As it was, like so many other people who have been raised in a tough environment, I was on a mission to make life better for myself. This was all I wanted—a slice of heaven that I wanted to claim and carve out for myself however I wanted. To be completely honest, I never spared much thought or cherished some prospect to become a millionaire, live in a large mansion or see the world from the suite balcony of a lavish cruise ship cabin. I wanted money, but just enough to be able to support myself and have a decent place to live in, nothing extraordinary. I was a city girl with a country girl's heart. I, quite simply, craved a happy family to spend my days and years with, a little world of love to call my own.

Quite understandably, these type of highly undesirable detours—my parents' divorce, failed relationship, and pregnancy—were never in my plans. Well, let's just say that the divorce and failed relationship were undesirable. My pregnancy, unbeknown to me, turned out to be the most sacred of blessings. A mother's heart is the source of all compassion and love. From it, beautiful things can stem, manifested in the relationship with one's children.

Back then, however, I was yet in the dark. In my still-tender years, I figured I was hurt badly twice in my life, two times too many. The first time was by my own parents because of their separation, and also because of all the issues I had to face by living in a broken home. The second time, it was my son's father who cleaved my heart in two and then smashed it into a million pieces. Again I stress that I was so young at the time, and I really did not understand the reason why all this had to happen to me. I keep saying this because, as could be expected, life taught me differently. Pain inevitably knocks on one's door, but the way one sees it and deals with it is a different matter entirely.

I think that, where my parents were concerned, one of the major problems that I had was that my mother and father never took the time to discuss with me why they were divorcing. I could sense the hurt that both my parents were going through during that cursed period, but they never involved their children in their travails or shared their innermost feelings with us. They shunned straightforwardness for the restrained propriety which many unhappy couples tended to adopt in those times, times when problems had to be swept under the carpet and the offending emotions shoved way deep inside, to be finally sealed, and denied, with a forced smile and even more false conversation. So when the bomb hit, we were completely unprepared. To the very day the puzzle dissolved, we had been completely left out from their world of pain and tribulations.

If there was one lesson I learned from this whole experience, it was to always include your child in the decision-making process, especially when the decisions that need to be made are ones that will have an impact in the child's life. It is never worth trading love and understanding for convention. It is the children's well-being that should count more than anything, not "how things look." Rules are vital, and there are some things that are meant only for the ears of adults; but sometimes, convention will not keep your children smiling and fill their hearts with happiness.

This family crisis that I went through at a young age left me feeling emptiness in my heart; and from it I carried an ugly void, which had eventually turned to anger, throughout my pregnancy. In addition, my disappointment in the unwholesome relationship I had created with my son's father did not make the situation any better.

Of course, when I got pregnant, I knew I had several choices. I had different places to go if I wanted to. I could have gone to Rochester, New

York, to live with relatives; or I could have decided to go back home. However, I decided to make it on my own in my city: New Orleans. I wanted to be independent, and this was the best way to make a fresh start in my mind. I didn't tell anyone in the family that I was pregnant. It was as though I wanted a clean break from the past.

I chose to move forward with my son and make the best out of whatever was available to me. I would not consider any other alternative which did not include my son living and growing up with me at his side. I strongly felt that the thing I really missed most in my life was love, and therefore, I realized I had been looking for it in all the wrong places. A broken home can be a devastating situation if you have no one to turn to, and now my world had changed even more dramatically. I had a life growing inside me, someone to take care of. It was a miracle. It wasn't simply about *me* any more. It was a terrifying sensation.

But life's challenges kept coming. One thing I haven't mentioned is that, one night before all this, our family home burned down to a crumbling shell. Luckily, we all came out of the blazing structure unscathed, including my dog, Duke. It was undoubtedly fortunate that my older brother was awakened by a strange dream, only to look into a dark cloud of smoke. As soon as he was lucid enough to realize what was happening, he jumped out of bed and rushed to wake up everybody and tell us we needed to get out of the house immediately.

A guardian angel was watching over him that day because, barely seconds after he got away from his bed, the fire spread to his sheets and mattress, destroying everything in its wake. The fire does not discriminate between animate and inanimate objects; it simply takes and turns things into ashes. There was no use beating around the bush—we had a close brush with death that day, and we were well aware of that fact. As a higher power willed it, however, within minutes, we were out of harm's way; but all our belongings were lost. Perhaps this is the reason why, after that day, I have cherished life itself more than any object or possession. I would rather lose a house or a car than be deprived of the air I breathe or of a loved one, and I wish the same for all the people of the world.

Later, when I faced more challenges with my son, I understood so much more about things. I had been raised in a sheltered life, but these new experiences made me look at everything from a whole new perspective. I think that I started to *understand* more, to realize why people do the things they do and react certain ways in particular situations.

That other day, however, four months into my pregnancy, as I waited for the bus, everything changed. A soft voice from up above spoke to me and told me, "Everything is going to be all right. You are carrying inside you a great athlete who will have the potential of becoming one of the greatest in the world." How I received that message, I cannot explain, but it was loud and clear as if I had been reading it from a book or listening to it on the radio.

I stood still for a few seconds, letting it all sink in. Then, all of a sudden, my tears stopped falling and I saw my life ahead. I never cried any more after that day. The bus arrived. As I escalated the steps of the hulking vehicle with the roaring motor, a thought struck me—the baby's father would rue the day he left when he finally realized what a treasure he helped create and then abandoned. And I knew that from that day forward, love would reign in my life. The real kind. The kind of love that we carry with us till the day we die. I was blessed.

My son was born on August 7, 1982, at Charity Hospital on Tulane Avenue. I could feel in my bones that my days would be filled with magic and his presence would give me purpose.

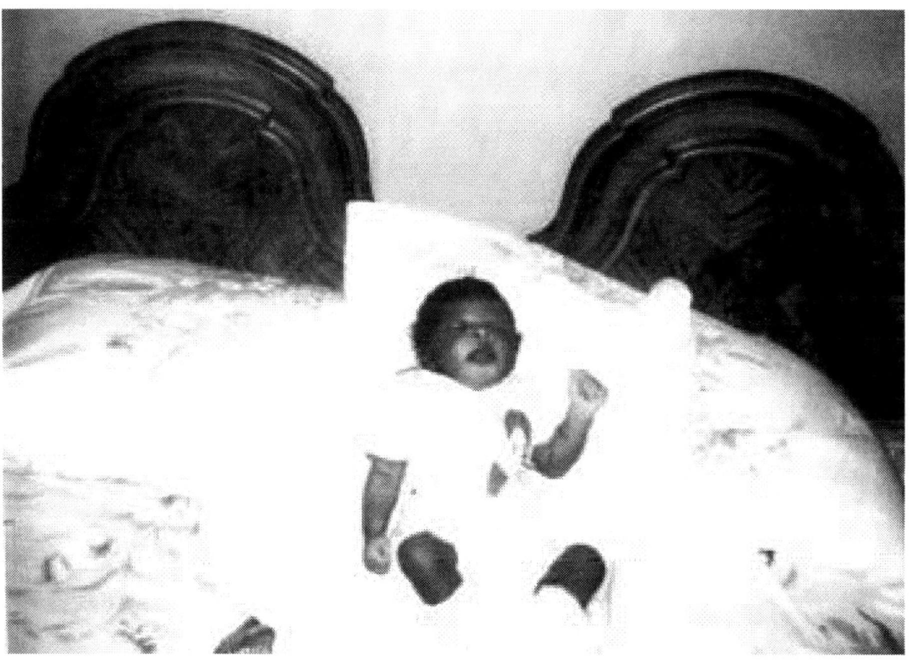

Marquise when he was one week old.
He grew at the lightning speed. After he was born,
I only used one box of *small* Pampers and the rest was history.

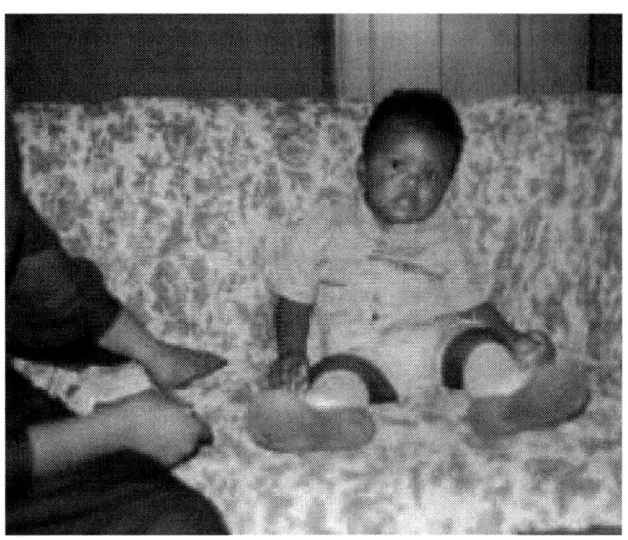

Marquise at 8 months wearing 2Ts.
Not long after this picture was taken he started walking.

MARQUISE YANNICK HILL

MY RECORD KEEPING WHILE MY SON WAS GROWING UP

WT AT BIRTH 8LBS 11OZ 21 INCHES LONG
NO SOFT SPOT IN THE MOLD OF HEAD AFTER THREE MONTHS
8 MONTHS HE WAS WEARING 2TS CLOTHES
BEGIN WALKING AT 8 MONTHS
AT AGE 1 SIZE OF 3 YR OLD
WAS RIDING A 10 SPEED AT 4 YEARS OLD
OVER 6FT BETWEEN 11 AND 12 YRS OLD
HT AT 13 YRS OLD 6'3 FEB 1995
HT AT 14 YRS OLD 6'5 ¾ THE DATE I MEASURED FEB 6 1996
HT AT 15 DOB 8-7-82 HT 6'6 DATE I MEASURED 8-17-1997
WEIGHT 271 LBS .... I WEIGHTED HIM ON THIS DATE ALSO 8-17-1997
WEIGHT LIFTING 150 LBS
SHIRT SIZE 3X
PANTS SIZE KHAKI STYLE 44-46 WAIST 34 LEG LENGTH

Record Sheet (growth chart) which survived Katrina.

II

A SINGLE PARENT

Because of the fact that I was away from home, life appeared—it was—difficult for me as a single parent. However, I was determined to make it through the bad times, no matter what. My son was born in August in 1982, about three years after I graduated from college. In more ways than one, I was luckier than most other girls who have to deal with a teenage pregnancy before they even have a clue what they wish to do with their lives.

Being somewhat older, I had a few more options. In order to get away from my family problems, and seeing that I had an opportunity to transfer my part-time job from Alabama, I felt compelled to move to New Orleans. Three years had passed since graduation and I wanted to explore other options in a larger city. I was old enough to do so, and I did. My plan was to work part-time while I learned my way around the new place and found a job in my field. Beyond this, I had no plan for the future other than continue my education once I was established, but I was determined to make it work . . . and this I also did. When I left home, I felt I was free to make my own decisions. But the unthinkable occurred—Marquise. If I could press a rewind button on my life I would replay it just to see my son again. But time has no rewind button. At that time, my family structure had crumbled and fallen apart and while I was in school, my support system had disappeared. I was on my own when I graduated. Nonetheless, when trouble knocks you down you get back up. My parents' divorce and the fire caused delays and bitterness. I was determined to be positive. I worked until Marquise was born.

In fact, my mother was not even aware of my expecting state until I was practically giving birth on the labor table in the hospital. I remember that back then, a friend of mine—Bonnie—contacted my mother because I was experiencing complications. I was in labor for over twenty-four hours.

This was the only reason I consented to get in touch with my mother at the time. I wouldn't open up to her or to anyone else, for that matter. That's just the kind of anger I was holding within me.

However, after a time, I realized that I did not have to be angry. I did not have to be afraid of not being accepted by my family, even more so because time heals and life goes on. I now had a son to raise, and I wanted things to be different for him—better than they had ever been for me. I would bring the sky down and make the stars dance for this little creature I held in my arms. After giving birth to my son, my mother immediately came to visit me and my baby boy for a week. It was as though some sort of truce had been formed, and after that time, we kept in touch.

My family wanted me to return home, but I refused. When Marquise was born, I was living with a friend—still in transition, working hard to find my own way. You may ask yourself: how did she graduate from college and live in a nice home, only to put herself in that situation? I have only one thing to say, things happen for a reason, and that reason for me was Marquise. I had to make it by myself, and I had to show my boy that we could be one little family. Nothing else mattered.

So I started from scratch and worked my way up. I was young, but I knew this much—anything could happen in life, and things would turn around in the blink of an eye. I took nothing for granted. I chose to live this life, and now, I choose to write about it. "If life gives you lemons, make lemonade"—one of Marquise's favorite sayings and one of the central tenets that helped us both push through life with determination, strength, and most of all, love.

After Marquise's birth, I had a job as a department store manager. It was a position with unstable hours; so it proved difficult to find and, more importantly, keep a babysitter. The first babysitter I hired, Marquise's first nanny, was called Mrs. Bernie (Bernice Horn was her full name)—a wonderful thirty-nine-year-old lady, a mature mother in her own right, with whom I felt comfortable leaving my son. She loved Marquise like he was one of her own. Her own children were aged seven and sixteen at the time, so she loved the thought of caring for a baby again. One thing I clearly remember about her is that she was always amazed at his size. She liked to tell me over and over, "This little guy is going to be a big one!"

Mrs. Bernie's daughter got married on June 1, 1984. I remember that this was Marquise's first public appearance in a white tuxedo, a tall bundle of not even two years of age! He made a bit of a scene because he didn't want to walk the aisle by himself as he was very shy and not one to enjoy giving public performances. All dressed up in his tux, he looked twice his age, and the people in the church couldn't believe his size when I told them just how old he was.

Marquise walking down the aisle at his nanny's daughter's wedding wearing a white tuxedo. This was his first public appearance. The wedding was held in June 1984. He was about to turn two on August 7.

My close friend, Yolanda, would also watch Marquise for me sometimes when I was unable to get a babysitter. To this day, whenever I speak to Yolanda, we laugh about how people could not believe my son's age since when he was six months old. He was huge, and he would always wear clothes that would normally fit a boy at least two years his senior. I only purchased one box of small Pampers when he was born. After that, I had no further use for this item as he just kept growing and growing until he literally jumped out of my lap when he reached the two-month milestone. Just to give you a clearer picture of things, I can say that he was so big that no child's diaper size would fit him. In fact, my only option was *Depends*! Luckily, I began potty training him early.

I also noticed another thing about Marquise: he was incredibly agile in his physical movements. As I observed him with a keen eye, I made sure he would develop his athletic abilities at a tender age, supervising his improvements at school and with his coaches. He turned out to be such a natural at sports, and I knew—I felt it in my heart and saw the proof in front of his eyes—that this was his calling.

I continued to make surprising discoveries about Marquise—each day was like a present waiting to be unwrapped. What will Marquise be up to this week? I would think. His skills, particularly the physical ones, were displayed effortlessly and never in a manner that was short of "amazing." For example, he was riding a regular ten-speed bike at barely four years of age! Nobody could say that this was the norm.

Going back to what I was about to say earlier, when Marquise was but a few months old, I was still without a stable job that would bring in substantial money for us to survive. It therefore started becoming increasingly difficult to afford a babysitter. My work shifts always changed because I was employed in the challenging and demanding position of a department store manager at the time. Especially before, during, and after the holidays, the hours would change; and there was no stability at all, no way to make long-term plans. Despite the help, therefore, it was tough to juggle the time with an unstable job.

A lack of dependable transportation also played a significant role with me finding a decent alternative job. Without a car, I had problems getting around; and being in a new city, I was not familiar enough with the area to feel comfortable. Many would even say that they would do anything to obtain a similar kind of job. Nonetheless, nobody could deny that balancing work hours with my duties as a single mother was no easy feat.

My mother, Marquise and I. He was very happy because he had stayed with my mother for a while in Alabama before she moved to New Orleans. This photograph was taken after her move. Marquise was one year old at the time.

All of these factors really made it difficult for me to get ahead with life. Things were especially tough during the Christmas holidays, when money was scarce and needs and wants, with a little boy in tow, were many and then some. However, I knew that somehow I would pull through.

And in fact, my prayers were finally answered. First, when Marquise was one year old, my brother came to take Marquise to my mother who had offered to take care of him while I focused on finding a more stable employment. Finally, in the summer, my mother made a decision. It so turned out that she was ready for a big change, so in June of 1983, she gave up her old home in Alabama and joined me in New Orleans to help me raise my son. I did not have to worry about going back and forth to the nursery anymore. By this time, our relationship was much improved. It seemed that Marquise's arrival brought sunshine in more than one respect—things acquired meaning, relationships were mended, attitudes were improved, and hopes were reborn. Finally, my brother Aaron helped me by giving me the use of an older but dependable car—just what I desperately needed!

Marquise and Tony the Tiger at Schwegmann's Supermarket in Gentilly. He was about four years old in this picture.

My mother's arrival was just another blessing for me. Later still, all of my brothers, with the exception of one, also moved to New Orleans. Once again, we were one big family; only this time things were so much better because we all created a new life in a new place, away from the bitter past memories of the events that had transpired in Alabama. With my mother's and brothers' help, my son was raised in the proper way, precluding the existence of two happily married parents—in a loving home, cherished by all who were close to him and bonded to him by blood.

I will never forget the day when I decided it was time to place Marquise in a nursery. My job was making significant demands on my time, and I needed some help. The incident I'm about to relate happened right around the time my mother was transitioning to New Orleans.

One day, I called the nursery director and gave her the necessary information over the phone, and she told me to take my documents to their office so that my son would be properly registered for child care. She did not ask to see the child prior to registration. He would start attending as early as the next day, and I could complete the registration process first thing when I brought him in. I remember her telling me that as he was only one year old, she would be able to place him in the room with other infants. I could have told her about Marquise's extraordinary appearance, but truly, I did not believe the information held much importance at the time.

When I arrived at the nursery the following day as scheduled, I could see the look of utter shock and amazement on her face when she laid eyes on Marquise. It was his sheer size, of course, that had the same effect on everyone. The lady quickly decided that she would have to place him with the two- and three-year-olds, rather than the infant peers. At one year of age, he was standing, somewhat proud and flat-footed with a bottle in his mouth, his body the size of a three-year-old.

She asked me what I fed him for him to become so big and so fast. I told her that he weighed eight pounds and eleven ounces at birth. He wore a size 2TS and started walking at eight months of age. At the age of three to four months, his head had no soft spot as all the other babies' heads do. I later learned what this meant—that his motor skills were already adequately developed this early, which made sense as it was pretty obvious he was, as I quickly discovered, born to be an athlete. One of the most extraordinary things I remember was when Marquise reached the whopping height of six feet when he was only eight years old! I made sure to keep a record of his growing pattern while he was going up.

Once my mother was situated in New Orleans, we made an arrangement where she would keep him while I was working, and I would do the same when she was working. My mother was in her late forties when she moved with us. Things were starting to get better for our family then. I started believing in that saying, "Good things come to those who wait." Or perhaps it was simply Marquise's baby charm, his innocence, his smile that were working their magic on the lives of those who came in close contact with him.

Thankfully, even my relationship with my father was being rekindled over the years, initially for Marquise's sake—and later for my own. After my parents' divorce, my dad remarried and stayed in Alabama. Later, he would help me provide for my son as best as he could. If he found out I was struggling, he would not hesitate to give me support. I am grateful to him for that; and thanks also to him, Marquise grew up to be a strong and healthy young man, surrounded by love and affection.

Our relationship was always positive. I never used his father's name or actions as a way to hurt or diminish him in any way. I wanted him to have a healthy self-esteem so he could become a man of principle when he grew up. We discussed things that mattered and resolved problems as a family.

Approximately a year or two after my mother's move to New Orleans, in 1984, my nephew, Dewayne—who was a son to my older brother, James (who sadly passed away in 2005 after Katrina), and whose mother lived in another state—joined our little family as well. At the time, Marquise was two years old; and my nephew, himself born in 1977, was seven. Despite the age discrepancy, when Dewayne first moved in, the two boys were of the same height. I still have a picture of them kneeling under the Christmas tree, taken about a year after Dewayne's move, attesting to this fact. Height was not an issue, however, where either boy was concerned.

Marquise and Dewayne under the Christmas tree celebrating the holidays for the first time together, a few months after Dewayne's transition to join our family.

My mother took custody of Dewayne because it was necessary due to a crisis occurring in his home life. My son was ecstatic that he had gained a sort of instant older brother to play and grow with. Dewayne's mother lived elsewhere, and Marquise had no father—they shared the same kind of deprivation in this regard. Marquise loved his cousin instantly, with the exuberance and sincerity only a child, or an adult with a child's heart, would display.

As the years passed and they grew together, my son was fast outgrowing Dewayne in size, so I had to make adjustments insofar as what chores to assign to whom. My nephew was about five years older than my son, granted, but soon Marquise was so much taller and stronger that I thought it would be fair to equally divide the chores between them. I also made sure to exercise fairness when I was giving gifts. If I went to the store and bought something for Marquise, I would also buy something to give to Dewayne. I treated them like brothers, like my sons, not simply as friends and playmates, because a brother is simply how Marquise saw Dewayne in his little boy's eyes. I would not shatter his young boy's perceptions because of pride.

Through Marquise's arrival, I could see my family getting together once more. He was my miracle. I have a family photograph that was taken during my brother's wedding in 1985. At the time, Marquise was three years old. He and Dewayne were outside playing when we took the picture. When I saw my entire family congregating to this place for this happy event, it felt like closure to me.

The last photo we had taken as a family before this day was when my parents had been celebrating their tenth anniversary—which was a long time past. This time, we took another picture as a family, despite the fact that our mother and father were not together any more. We were finally communicating as we should have been, and we found closure together. My main regret is that Marquise and Dewayne were not in that picture—above all, without my son being immortalized there, at that important moment, something appears to be missing.

A portrait I requested because this was the first time all the family had come together since my parent's divorce. To me it was closure—the beginning of a new chapter in our lives. Since this portrait I have lost one sibling after Katrina (far right).
At the time we took the photo, Marquise was about 3 years old, and he was outside playing with his cousin Dewayne. This was my brother's wedding (the one on the far left, second row). Marquise's grandparents, uncles and mother (me).

Marquise with his kindergarten class at Littlewoods Elementary School. Of course, he's one of the tallest in his class.

Wherever Marquise went, he was always the tallest kid, without exception. After the nursery incident, I managed to get a job teaching, so I planned to get him in pre-K after my first year on the new job. And I did manage to do that in my second year at work, just as planned—I enrolled Marquise in a school called Our Lady Star of the Sea. During the Christmas season that year, he played his first role in a Christmas play where he had a singing part, a five—to ten-minute skit, toward the end of the play. Everybody was amazed when they saw him onstage. He couldn't fail to stand out that time either. I remember how both parents and teachers were talking about it when the performance ended. There was no denying that he towered above all the other kids. It was uncanny, but for me, it was also a miracle.

So this was how Marquise and Dewayne grew up together. But unlike Dewayne, Marquise always had to face challenges because of his height. Sometimes, Dewayne was the source of those challenges; or perhaps, he was too afraid to lose the respect and companionship of his peers to be a source of support for Marquise. Dewayne was a good kid who was nonetheless facing problems of his own, and it is not a big secret that at that age, when young adulthood is knocking on our door, life is all about acceptance from others.

My brother recently reminded me of one incident that happened back in 1991 when Marquise came home crying from his trip to the park because Dewayne wouldn't let him play football with him and the other neighborhood kids. He was devastated at the rejection, especially because it came from his closest companion and brother. So my own brother, Danny, promptly walked back with him to the park and asked Dewayne to tell him why they wouldn't let his little cousin play. Dewayne reported that the other kids had said that Marquise was too big and clumsy and they didn't want him on their kids' team.

As could perhaps be expected, Marquise learned early on the disadvantages of his hulking size. He was either shunned or overly scrutinized. Either way, he was distressed by the situation. Sometimes, the unwanted attention disturbed him, being shy as he was. Other times, he thought nothing of it. It got better as he grew older and he learned to use his appearance to his advantage. He would not retreat into a shell anymore, at the expense of anything he could choose to be. He realized that his athletic frame and prowess were a gift from above that had to be molded and nourished, not wasted because of undesirable, negative emotions that can only hold a person back in life.

Many years later, when he was seventeen years old, I was working at a juvenile correctional facility. The officers used to tease him about how large he was, and they would tell him how glad they felt that he wasn't one of the juveniles they had to deal or wrestle with. He would laugh at their good-natured taunts, and I'm sure he told himself how grateful he was that he had grown with a good head on his shoulders. He had the good sense to be appreciative of what he had received, which is what I had hoped and sensed would one day happen.

The amazing thing was that he always had a baby face, even when he was all grown up. People would say he was going to be another Shaq, and hardly a day passed as he grew from a boy into a young adult that someone wouldn't comment about his age or size. Since he turned twelve, people would tell me, "That kid is going to make you some money one day." This statement started to sound like a broken record. And admittedly, perhaps this perception of others made him feel more pressured to succeed and prove them right.

III

HIS FIRST ENCOUNTERS WITH DEATH

My nephew and his other friends came to me one day and told me that Marquise had been hit by a car. Marquise was about four years old at the time. When I recovered from the shock, I asked to see my son and demanded that they tell me what had happened. Apparently, Marquise was riding a bicycle and the driver did not see him coming. When my son realized the car was about to crash into him, it was too late. He was hit before anyone could stop him.

Angry and overwhelmed by what had just happened, Marquise jumped up from under the car and grabbed the driver by her hair. His shock had apparently stopped his brain from functioning. He was livid and distressed, and he felt that the woman had almost killed him when she could have avoided the entire accident just by being a little more careful. Nonetheless, I later expended much energy to drum into him that what he did was wrong, that he shouldn't have reacted that way.

He had so much anger in him that my nephew and his friends had to pry him away from her and calm him down. My son said to me later that all he could see was the car approaching; and in a flash, before he could move away, he was thrown off his bike and underneath the car. He never told me all the details until he was older because he knew what my instructions to him always were "to stay out of the streets and stick to the driveway while riding a bicycle." For reasons anyone could guess, I never had to worry about him being in the streets on a bicycle again. Marquise was a fast learner.

Apartment before Katrina. Marquise and a playmate, Michael, at Curran Place Apartments, the complex where we lived until I was more financially stable. He began riding a 10 speed when he was 4 years old.

The park where Marquise played many times was right down the street, not far from our apartment.

Curran Place after Katrina. This apartment complex is now condemned. I moved out in the late 80's.

But this, I was later to find out, was not the biggest threat my boy would face in life. During his kindergarten days through fifth grade, we lived in an apartment complex that was subsidized by the government. I had originally taken the apartment (Curran Place, it was called; it is currently uninhabitable as it was razed by Katrina) because as I have explained earlier on, I found it was hard to find a stable job without valid transportation in the eighties and nineties, especially if you were not politically connected to the right person. So the concept of living in this complex worked out advantageously for me as I was a single parent, and if I ever happened to lose my job, paying the rent would not be a concern.

The place was brand-new at that time, and the apartment came complete with central air and heat—something I would have considered a luxury back then. That made me feel a little more secure and comfortable in the possibility of raising my son there, but I knew I would never accept the idea of staying in that place forever as it was not part of my long-term goals to live this way. I had never lived in subsidized housing before in my life, and the whole experience turned out to be a culture shock to me.

For Marquise, it was a different outlook and experience as he was still pretty much a baby—he had nothing else to compare it with. Notwithstanding, I had learned long before that one has to accept the challenges life dishes out. I believed in the maxim I adapted for myself, "If you make your bed hard, you have to lie in it."

Before this time, I had never had anything to say either against or in favor of subsidized housing; it was something entirely new to me, coming from a family who had never depended on any housing program. As I have already stated, I had lived with a friend of mine for a while, prior to getting pregnant until after my son was born; then, when Marquise was a little over one year old, I moved on to this particular apartment complex in the east. The place was called Littlewoods, and the move heralded the start of a new life for me and my baby. My father had always provided for our family; and this state of affairs, coming after living out a modest but comfortable existence, made it all the more devastating when my parents' separation came into play. It was the first time I knew real poverty and had to deal with it for many years thereafter.

As the years passed while I lived life in my new apartment, the area around Curran Place changed or, much rather, it deteriorated. Drug dealing and loud music abounded to an alarming degree. In 1984, I began teaching at a private school; and a few years later, I took a job as a preschool center supervisor. During this time—between 1990 and 1994—the murder rate had escalated to an all-time high in New Orleans. Over four hundred murders a year occurred from 1990 through 1995—more murders occurred than the number of days in a year. I witnessed my first murder scene while working in the Desire Projects; then, later that month, I saw the results of two other murders that had been committed in broad daylight.

Marquise and I standing outside looking at how the area was beginning to deteriorate because of drug use and crime.

This was an experience that most people never dream of getting close to, and this is the environment surrounding Marquise's first years. Dewayne was also with us at that time, soaking in these scenes like a sponge. These things were happening right there, close to me, on my job site. So anyone can imagine what kind of crime was going on in the city. I was determined to keep Marquise and Dewayne walking on the right side of the fence, and I knew that would be my biggest challenge. Marquise was a sensitive child; and any deterioration in his behavior, had it ever happened, would have been devastating to him above all others.

To illustrate just how sensitive he was, I would like to mention an incident that happened a little after this period, in 1996, when Marquise had turned fourteen years of age. By that time, he was already standing six feet five, and we had just moved into a new apartment. Financial resources were low and, sometimes, unpredictable due to unforeseen bills or the like. Christmas was just around the corner, and I wasn't sure how we would plow through it.

I remember sitting him down and trying to explain my financial problems to him. I told him, "Ma feels that it would be better to just get your Christmas presents right after Christmas because it would be much cheaper. Would that be OK for you?"

His response was, "Yes, Ma." However, I wasn't sure if he really understood the implications of what I had told him—that is, that he wouldn't be getting his chosen presents on time that year. So I explained the situation about Santa Claus, and he looked at me with wide, all-too-serious eyes when I was talking to him. Until Marquise's passing in May, we would sometimes remember this story and start laughing; but back then, it was a serious matter to him.

So lo and behold, my son woke up on Christmas Day, saw no presents under the tree, and broke down crying. He cried so effusively, as if he had failed a test at school. I was totally distraught. Here was this child, standing so big and tall, falling out because he found no Christmas toys under the tree. I never tried that any more, but really I didn't have to, as Marquise was well on his way to young adulthood.

After watching his distress, I gave him a $200 check for Christmas, as I figured anything would stop him from crying at that point. It worked, and I saw his face light up, thinking about the new stuff he would get. Like any kid, he enjoyed all toys, games, and bikes. I remember purchasing so many bikes during his childhood because he kept breaking them due to his size. They would only last a few weeks after which the wheel would bend or break. One day, feeling totally exasperated after he broke yet another of his bikes, I informed him that I was through buying more for him unless I could find one made of steel.

So in regard to the Christmas incident, in my mind, I thought that, as he was mature enough to understand the facts of life, something as small as holding off on toys would not have affected him so much. I was so wrong. His body had truly outgrown his maturity, and I had forgotten just how sensitive he was deep down. He never stopped being sensitive, but as he grew older, he channeled this emotion more positively.

Knowing just how emotional he was, I always strove to make sure he stayed on track. Back in those days, in that situation and those hard times, it was me against the rest of the world—and I would be the anchor that would prevent him from losing his way. It was a learning experience for me as much as it was for him, but I was adamant not to lose this battle. I wanted to teach him to walk on the straight and narrow, to let him know that he could not compromise where his life was concerned. There was no middle ground in these matters.

One late afternoon when Marquise was eight or nine years old, the streets showed him how bad things could be. He and my nephew were walking home in East New Orleans from the corner store, and all of a sudden, they heard a series of gunshots being fired in what sounded like an ambush. Marquise and my nephew came home scared, telling me they thought that a murder had just occurred down the street. I had just been about to take a nap, but I decided that I had to go and see what was going on.

I was very upset over the whole incident, especially knowing that Marquise and Dewayne were walking home from the store when the shooting happened. There was no telling what could have happened—a stray bullet could have struck any one of them and killed them in an instant. This time, they could have been the ones who ended up "in the wrong place at the wrong time." Sometimes it seems that no place is truly safe, not even one's own home. On that note, I recently read about a 2007 incident in Arizona where a little girl was killed by a stray bullet which burst through the window of her room while she was quietly doing her homework on the computer. Another stray bullet also killed two people—a lady and a child—this year (2008) on New Year's Day in Atlanta, Georgia.

Marquise and Dewayne under the breezeway close to the time when they witnessed a murder scene. They experienced a lot of changes in the neighborhood during this period.

While most people were celebrating or comfortably settled in their homes after an evening of revelry, these individuals had to face tragedy. I cannot imagine the anguish these families are feeling. Perhaps I do, but in different ways. What mostly comes to my mind when I read of these incidents is, what is the world coming to?

As we walked toward the murder scene, I could see the devastation in both my son's and nephew's eyes. I knew they had never witnessed anything like this before, and I hated that they had to be exposed to this horror. My son knew the victim, which made the whole event even more devastating and surreal. Once we reached the scene, the body was lying in the street, the marred flesh of the young man ruthlessly barreled with several gunshot wounds. The body was literally drowning in blood. It was the body of a twenty-two-year-old drug dealer who had been targeted for murder.

In that moment, I turned to the kids and said to them, "This is what drugs and drinking will do for you. They will either put you in jail or land you in the cemetery. You have only these two choices available to you when you take this route—death or prison."

For several years after that fateful day, my son told me several times that he suffered nightmares about that incident and he could not get it out of his mind. He would always tell me that to him, it was like time hadn't passed and the memory just wouldn't fade away. He was stricken by images of death, flesh torn by lead.

He would tell me, "Momma, I remember everything the man was wearing. Drugs aren't for me."

He had made up his mind then and there that he would stay away from both drugs and drinking. From the time he was in kindergarten to the first grade, I never had any concerns about Marquise doing anything like that or of him accepting a tempting offer meant to lure him into a life of crime and sordid deals. He did not break his promise to me. My heart was full with gratefulness and pride.

Throughout his life, Marquise witnessed two murders. One day he turned to me and told me, "Will I live to see twenty-one?"

Of course, I reassured him that if he worked hard and lived his life positively, he didn't have to worry about all that. Today, that question he posed to me rings in my mind, and the near truthfulness of it gives me strong emotions. Yes, he did live to see twenty-one, but only barely, I think. But when my thoughts turn to dark, I lift them toward God and let him guide me back toward daylight.

Luckily for all of us, but most importantly for himself, he truly enjoyed school and learning. The process of discovery fascinated him to no end, and during this period, he never got in trouble. Later, his wholesome attitude endeared him to all who came in contact with him; and to some he even became a hero, especially in Katrina's aftermath. He never forgot his roots, notwithstanding all his successes and peoples' perception of him as a larger-than-life sort of person, which would make the average man blind to his past.

However, we did have to face some dark moments in Marquise's childhood and young adulthood. When he made it to the second grade, I began to notice a change in his behavior, although I couldn't quite put a finger on what it was. He told me once that his teacher had hit him. I attended PTA meetings all the time, and on this particular instance, I questioned the hitting incident to the teacher; but she denied it. I started getting reports from the teacher saying that my son was misbehaving and disrupting the class. To me, this seemed unusual as he was such a good, obedient kid at home. Was I raising Dr. Jekyll and Mr. Hyde? There was not much likelihood of that, I thought.

To my even deeper amazement, the teacher suggested that it would be best for him to repeat the second grade. Being an educator myself, I know how sometimes children are slow with catching on, and it is often best to correct a problem if it is detected in time while the children are in the lower grades. It was obvious that my son was afraid of telling me what really happened when he was in the second grade, so he went along with the suggestion of repeating the second grade and moving forward from there.

As time passed, I noticed that Marquise's self-esteem was declining, so I started watching him more closely and encouraging him to work on his confidence level. I could not have found words to express my relief. I was aware that children rebound quickly from their disappointments, but when one is a parent, it is difficult to set aside the worry. I let him know that he could be an A student if he put his mind to it and that I wasn't expecting anything less because I had no doubt he could succeed. It took much hard work, but I would soon come to see a marked improvement in things.

I helped him with his projects and his studies, and I would make sure he was doing it right and submitting his work on time. My efforts were constant, unrelenting, because I knew Marquise's potential and wouldn't settle for less. As always, he did not disappoint me or himself. For two years in a row, he won second and third place in the school project contest; and of course, he was very proud of himself as I was of him. It was a big deal for him, and I had saved a copy of the photo where he was holding his prize so he could reflect back on it in the later years. Unfortunately, I lost this photo, along with many other cherished mementos, in the Katrina disaster. Today, this story rests in my memory; it is one of those tender moments I will not forget.

As time went by, his confidence, along with his grades, began to gradually build up to the level where it was supposed to be. His new teacher was also wonderful, and he started collecting academic achievements and awards. I made it a point to interact with the teacher on a weekly basis to make sure he didn't repeat what he went through in the second grade again—despite the fact that I was not yet aware of the details.

I remember him talking about his favorite new teacher, Ms. Jet, all the time; and it was very obvious that he was really enjoying second grade this time around. This, again, made me think a few thoughts about his former second-grade teacher; but I decided not to bring up the incident again.

He continued working hard in school through the fifth grade. In the later year, there were only a few minor problems which saw me taking a few trips to the school—but it was never anything major. But then, right after graduation from the fifth grade—that's when he dropped the bomb on me.

Marquise at age eight. At this time I was teaching 5th, 6th, 7th and 8th grade Social Studies at St. Phillip Middle School. By this time, we had moved out of the first apartment because of the crime problem.

IV

WHEN HE DROPPED THE BOMB ON ME

When he was up for graduation from the fifth grade, he dropped the bomb on me. I was so hurt and disappointed by the revelation that I blamed myself for a long time for what happened. Before graduation, I had decided to remove him from his school and place him in a private school that was set up to help disadvantaged young black males at risk. I assumed that this move to a new, healthier environment would be beneficial for him.

Marquise attending his Big Mom's surprise 60th birthday party. Marquise was twelve years old at the time.

The crime level was so high at the time, and each day we were losing countless black males to a terrible life—or death—on our streets. I informed the school at the end of the year that my son would not be returning the following year. I explained my motivation for this—stressing on the fact that it would be good for him to attend a new school at this point, primarily because of the abovementioned reasons.

But on our way from home after the graduation ceremony that year, my son made a confession to me. It was a strange and devastating conversation, and it still pains me to remember it.

It was a warm day in New Orleans, and the sun was smiling over the city, embracing it with loving tendrils of light. This pretty picture made as if to tell me that what was to come would be as unexpected as a bolt of lightning in the sunshine. Marquise had just finished another year of school, and things were looking up. He had a new life to look forward to, and I felt content as I drove us toward our home. I had no reason to hold any reservations.

However, my peace was destined to be short-lived that day.

About a fourth of the way to our destination, he suddenly turned to me and said, "Ma, do you remember when I told you that my teacher hit me a few years ago?"

"Yes, I do," I replied. I remember stiffening in my seat because I felt he was on the verge of shedding some light on that mystery. "What about it?" I responded, vying hard for nonchalance and barely succeeding.

I should have known from the expression on his face that nothing good was about to come out of his mouth. In a low tone, he told me, "I must confess and tell you the truth. I feel so bad for not telling you."

"Keep going," I urged him. Again, I could feel my whole body tighten with dreaded tension, and my fingers gripped the steering wheel.

He nodded and continued.

"One day, I was out at recess playing with my spinning top, and another student was bothering me. He kept trying to take my spinning top. I told the teacher about it, like you always tell me to do. But the teacher did not do anything to take control of the situation, and the next thing I knew, the boy and I were fighting. The recess ended, and when I returned to the classroom, the teacher punched me in the side with the ring on her finger, and I felt and smelled blood trickling down under my clothes. So I caged her and threw a school chair on top of her head."

I had never seen any bruising or cuts, of course, because it was hidden under his clothing. I thought that if it had been anywhere visible, I would have most probably believed that it was the product of a classroom brawl between two hotheaded kids.

As the car cruised down the semideserted road, I could hardly register what he was telling me, and I almost cut a U-turn and drove back to the school in rage. However, I swallowed my anger, counted to ten, told myself to keep calm, and encouraged him to keep relating his story instead. His voice trembled and I could sense his fear, so I did not want to do or say anything to prevent him from telling me everything.

"I panicked and started running toward home from school," he continued. "All the way home, I ran the whole two miles. When I got home, I stuffed clothes in my pants because I knew you were going to kill me with a belt when the school called to tell you about the fight. I wanted the layers of clothes to dull the pain. I wanted to be prepared for anything."

Just the idea that he thought I would have harmed him or turned him out made my blood boil, but I kept my silence. I forced myself to think coherently. One thing I did remember was that no one had called me from the school or notified me of the incident. Why did I not think back then how strange that was? How inappropriate!

I must have been blind to brush it all off and move on as if nothing had happened. The sad part was that I hadn't given it much thought, and for me, everything had been business as usual as I had no idea what had happened the previous day—and my son would not say anything because he feared what I would do if I found out about the incident. At that point, I asked him to tell me exactly what had happened and to be entirely truthful this time.

Marquise just graduated from 5th grade.
Marquise (at age 13) and I. This photo was taken around the time he "dropped the bomb on me."

He told me that the assistant principal had called him into his office and asked him to relate what had happened in the classroom and then instructed him to return to class. That was when the teacher told him to move to the corner and stay there. He was treated like he had behavioral problems and made to feel like he was different from everyone else. To my horror, he even confessed that the teacher brought an older boy to the classroom—a relative or friend who was also a big boy—to position him as a sort of threat to Marquise. My son rebelled to this treatment and told his teacher that if she wanted her son to avoid getting in a fight, she would do better to leave him alone.

So many things started falling into place then, just like the pieces of a convoluted puzzle. For the rest of that year, Marquise was very likely picked on or marked as a troublemaker while I continued to be clueless. Everything made much more sense—his behavior during that time, especially—and this new discovery explained the change I had detected in him throughout the second grade. A change I could not quite put my finger on or figure out until this day. I remembered the strange looks and reactions from certain teachers or individuals at the school. At the time, it was all anathema to me.

When Marquise finally told me the whole story, the real version of the event, I felt myself becoming increasingly angry both with myself and him. I gave myself the blame because I didn't investigate the situation more thoroughly, and I was upset with my son because if he had been forthright from the beginning, things may have been so much different. I asked my nephew, who was privy to the whole thing, about it; and he corroborated everything my son had just told me.

I even confronted his former teacher, who unhesitantly denied that such a thing had ever happened. This means that nothing would ever be done to rectify the situation and to satisfy justice. The teacher would not be reprimanded and get her due. It was very likely that she had done the same thing to other children, perhaps she still does.

The school had been going through many changes, but it seemed that some were not for the better. I could not fail my son. I had to give him the benefit of the doubt. In fact, there is no uncertainty in my mind that everything he said to me that day was true. But if there was one good thing that came out of it since that time, it was that Marquise learned to manage all crises with a good deal more common sense. He never got into trouble at school from that day forward; he was never disciplined or suspended for any reason.

The next year, Marquise moved on to a different school.

After the confession as to what had happened in second grade, Marquise began to ask more questions about his father and wondering why his father was not living with us at home. Seeing his innocent curiosity and longing to know more about his dad, I decided to put all my anger aside and said to myself that if Marquise's father did not care, he could at least pretend to do so. I thought that if the man didn't care for his son, he will one day have to answer for it, and it wasn't my place to judge him. As my grandmother and parents always said, "What goes in the washing comes out in the rinsing." What goes around comes around.

I was not averse to the idea of Marquise having a relationship with his dad. However, I never once thought of starting an active search for him—I thought if something was meant to be, then it would happen.

One day, as fate would have it, I bumped into him by sheer coincidence, and he told me he wanted to see our son. Our meeting could not have happened at a better time. I gave him the number and address and told him he could visit the following week.

I prepared Marquise for his father's arrival, and the boy was so excited he was beside himself. On the day of the visit, I prayed that he would not be disappointed with this experience, and his innocent happiness brought tears to my eyes. Unfortunately, my fears were not unfounded. Marquise's father came over on time for the appointment, at which time he immediately proceeded to manufacture lies to impart to my son—lies cumulating in false promises and empty excuses—which made things so much worse for me.

Their day started with them talking in my living room. After a while, he took Marquise to the corner store to buy him a soda. When Marquise asked if he could have chips, he refused to buy him a bag—the reason for which I cannot fathom to this day. The only thing I know is that his father, whom he had never seen before in his life, refused to purchase a mere bag of chips for his own son!

Then, even worse, he promised him he would get him something for Christmas and that he would give him money as well. The coup de grace came when he told him that they would be spending a lot of time together as father and son. This was the most terrible lie because, sadly, Marquise never heard from his father again.

My son was very angry for a long time, and he held his rage inside him like a trapped lion in a tight cage. There is no doubt that the biggest lie—I soon discovered—was his father telling him that he could call any time; but when he did just that, the given phone number was disconnected. There was no other way for Marquise to contact his dad because he had not provided us with a physical address. Hence, from then on, my son regrouped and decided to write his dad out of his life.

His prior belief that his daddy was away working and couldn't visit had turned into lies and more lies. When he was one- to six-years old, I would tell him that his father was working out of state; and to ease the blow of not having a dad around, I did my utmost to fill the position of father figure. At the same time, I did not want him to hate his dad. One may think I also lied to him, but my intent was to spare him—not give him—pain.

I felt that this encounter with his real father set me back ten years, and all the work I did with Marquise in this regard was unraveled in the blink of an eye. After this incident, he stopped asking questions about his father. The next time my son heard from him was when he was about to enter college. By this time, incidentally, his football career was taking off and his name was in the limelight. The phone rang one day, and when Marquise heard that dreaded voice of shattered dreams on the other line, he poured all his anger and hurt. He spared no quarter and made sure his father knew how much his treatment had stung. After saying what he had to say, Marquise hung up the receiver without uttering a word in response.

Around this time, I bought the book about Dr. Ben Carson, *Gifted Hands*, and showed it to Marquise so he could read it and learn from it. We decided to read it together; and when we were done, we discussed the struggles he had encountered, including his experience with his father and how the lessons garnered from the book would give him insight into his own situation. I was pleased to hear him say that he wouldn't let it stop him, that life was an obstacle course fraught with hurdles, but he would jump over them and move forward toward his dreams.

Sometime later, we had the good fortune to watch and hear Ben Carson speak at the SUNO (Southern University in New Orleans) graduation ceremony at the UNO Lakefront Arena. It was an unforgettable experience!

I was happy to watch my son gain confidence in himself and find constructive ways to deal with his pain. His heart full of vigor and promise, Marquise said to me, "If Dr. Carson can make it, then I know I can make it too."

And so his prophetic words stayed with me a long time, and when his star started shining, I remembered them fondly and held them close to my heart.

Going back to the incident at the school and the period following Marquise's bitter experience with his father, I felt I needed to take action and pull our lives together. Things were getting out of hand and going in the wrong direction, and deceit and lies were coming into play. Once we take a road of deception, it is hard to go back, and most likely one lie will lead to another. I could not see how this had slipped by me. I wanted to teach Marquise the real meaning of family, to feel that he could always depend on his loved ones, so I began to monitor him closely to make sure that anything of the sort would not happen again.

I administered a sort of tough love. I would show up at school unannounced, volunteer in various activities, and participate in the PTA. Armed with the knowledge of what had happened in elementary school, I began to check on him weekly and sometimes daily. The fact that one of Marquise's old nannies, Mrs. Bowman, and a teacher, Mr. Wells, worked at the Fannie C. Williams Middle School was a huge plus. I had a couple of allies who were ready and willing to help me keep a tight lid on my son.

When Marquise was in the sixth grade in a new school he was attending catering mostly to disadvantaged black males, a teacher cursed him out while the principal was standing right there in the classroom, listening and watching. I had walked into this tableau; so I questioned the situation and asked my son—now a six-foot-tall hulking giant—to tell me, truthfully, what had happened. I certainly did not want history to repeat itself. He explained all that had happened; and upon further investigation, it turned out that my son had a right to complain, and it was unacceptable that he had to be treated so crudely by his own teacher. I demanded that they explain such behavior, and the school claimed they would look into the incident.

"Cursing out" of a student by a teacher or any member of staff within an educational institution would be regarded in any case as totally unacceptable behavior. The story was that the teacher was allowing one student to take a test over, but not the whole class. Therefore, my son told him that he could not just sit and take the test again because it was unfair to the other students. Falling into a rage upon hearing Marquise's outburst, the teacher cursed my son right in front of the principal!

But this time, I knew that my son would not stand for anything he felt was unjust, and he started speaking out about different things. He expressed his hurt like he didn't do the first time when the second-grade teacher had hit him. Marquise was now older and had learned a most valuable lesson. This time, I was able to question the incident immediately and demand that something be done. Sadly, I was given nothing but excuses.

However, the thing that happened after I started probing into this incident was that I received an odd letter from the school informing me that it would be better for all involved if I sent Marquise to a different school. Marquise had never been suspended for getting in trouble, and they would not give me a reason for their decision.

I called the school several times to discuss their less-than-courteous communication; but no one bothered to return my call—whether this was intentional or otherwise, I cannot surely say, but I am inclined to believe it was. Whatever the reason was for the school's stance, one cannot deny that the administration's attitude and blunt message was entirely unprofessional.

Marquise's second confession to me after the sixth grade strengthened my resolve to move him to yet a better environment in a different school. I was convinced it was all for the best. If I had any doubts about it before I received the letter from the school, they quickly dissipated. It was time for another move—one I didn't regret. I was yet to find a school where Marquise could be treated as an equal to the others in his class, and I was sure the next one would be it. And I was right—Fannie C. Williams happened to be a great place. There, as mentioned above, I made lots of allies who would help me keep Marquise on the straight and narrow. Mrs. Bowman, Mr. Wells, even the security guard, Maurice—these were Marquise's guardian angels.

Marquise took these developments in stride. Despite the challenges we faced, I can safely say that I was fortunate and blessed nonetheless because God surrounded me with good-hearted people at a time when I needed the most help.

V

FINDING THE WAY THROUGH A MAZE

I found it hard to deny Marquise anything after all he had been through at school and in life. I would soon discover that this was not a good thing. The time came when my son wanted a dog—and really, which child doesn't? The chow with the purple tongue happened to be his favorite. So I purchased a solid black puppy, and he named him Shaq.

The dog he wanted so badly. He named him "Shaq."
I finally had to move to an apartment house with a fence for safety reasons.

Shaq was beautiful while he was a puppy, but as he got older, he became more and more aggressive. It was a bad decision because for a dog this size, I needed my own yard, a space my home definitely lacked. At the time I purchased him, I only had a little patio, which was not a lot of space. Because of this discomfiting aggressive trait, my son's interest in taking care of his pet rapidly diminished, except for short moments when he felt like playing with the household pet. Then again, it is fairly common for children to stop their pet-caring duties after finding out about the amount of work involved. Marquise, being the typical child, also came to join this crowd. Hence, Shaq became my dog.

I made a lot of research on this type of animal and discovered that chows are territorial dogs; they do not like to share their space with strangers. My son did not like this particular aspect of the dog's character, and he was tired of Shaq biting his friends. One of his friend's parents reported such an incident to the apartment community management; and because of this, rather than give up my dog with which I was now deeply attached, I felt compelled to move to a different house because of liability issues. The apartment complex from which I had to move was a nice new unit located in East New Orleans. I would not have left were it not for this tricky situation.

In the meantime, a friend of my brother held Shaq in her backyard for me until I was able to do something with the dog. Both Marquise and I had access to the backyard. During that time, he bit both my nephew and my mother. We began to think that Shaq felt abandoned by us because, prior to this, he had not attacked anybody in our family.

Later, my son was given another puppy, a Doberman pinscher. I was very upset with him because now I had two dogs of different breeds to take care of. Shaq's behavior worsened, and predictably my son would not perform his dog-caring chores properly. It would often fall on me to feed them and do all the other necessary things that one would do for a pet.

One evening, I went over to the backyard to feed Shaq, and he bit me. It was late, and my brother had to take me to the hospital. By the time my son received word of the incident, he was told that Shaq had almost bit my arm off. Marquise was sick with worry and reacted in a most alarming way.

Later, he told me how he felt he had turned into Hulk and was so out of control. He told me, "I ran about a mile in two seconds!" And to be honest, he wasn't too far from the truth. That boy could outrun the speed of light. This was how we all discovered his running ability. He jumped the eight-foot fence into the backyard where Shaq was located with nary a thought. The dog was so startled that it jumped out of the yard over the fence in reaction.

We therefore decided to take the dog to the SPCA. They told us that they'd keep him for two weeks, after which they'd put him to sleep. I had to call them to talk them out of putting the dog down because Shaq was in a rage and thus a considered danger to people. Incidentally, after a few days, my brother's friend and coworker asked us if we would let him adopt Shaq; and we accepted in order to avoid having to euthanize our pet. As protection for my family, I had the gentleman sign papers confirming that he was aware of the dog being dangerous and that he released me of all liability in the event of any undesirable accidents happening. Shaq's new owner stated that he would take the dog to his home in the country where the animal would not be able to hurt anyone. Despite his assurances, I was not comfortable with this decision. First of all, I hated the idea of giving Shaq up. Secondly, I was not such a fool as to think that his aggressiveness would not resurface, even in a country setting.

Unfortunately, my misgivings were warranted because Shaq struck again, and this time he had to be put down. I was very upset, and I cried all day when I heard the news. I loved Shaq so much and didn't want him to meet this grisly end. Despite Marquise's deceivingly apparent lack of affection for Shaq, he did care and he was also heartbroken about the situation.

I learned a lot from this episode. I should have done my research before purchasing this dog. Rather than succumb to Marquise's wishes, I should have let common sense rule, and I would have realized my home was not big enough for a dog of such considerable size. I had to move into a house with a fenced yard so I could accommodate the dog that my son did not want to take care of anymore. My point is, it is more important to get your children what they need rather than what they want. However, I firmly believe that God always provides us with answers, sometimes in a most unconventional way . . . but he always sends clues.

During this time, I had recovered my faith. Sometime earlier—in fact, after going through many trials and tribulations such as trying to find a better place to live when the crime rate was so high, a stable job, and yes, even when I so desired to have a faithful companion to help raise my son—I had decided to turn my life to Jesus. As I always say, this decision definitely worked out for me. He worked out for me.

I started attending Greater St. Stephen Baptist Church, but I did not officially join until 1991 because I had been raised in the Pentecostal faith. Back in Alabama, I used to attend the Allen Temple. However, during this time, a new movement was on the rise with this church; and I found that it was the answer to what I had been looking for. I was searching for the Word of God and wasn't really keen on being a part of a specific denomination. I did not want recognition of who I was. I just wanted to live for Jesus and the Word and keep the courage to move forward in my life.

This church and this faith were what helped me through the bad times. After I joined, my mother and Marquise also followed suit—the latter while he was in middle school. Like me, he never wanted the praise or the crowds or other peoples' recognition. He recognized the rewards of living a simple life and doing God's work. It was another proud moment for me as a mother to watch Marquise doing what felt so right.

After witnessing the harsh realities of life, he was always aware that one's freedom can be snatched away at any minute. He felt he had no minute to waste making mistakes and taking the wrong decisions. Life was too short. It was how he was and how he lived. Eventually, it was how he died.

Going way back to the crisis I had with my parents' divorce, I got somewhat offtrack with my roots. After joining the church, it was like going back home. Before I took this step, I sometimes had doubts about the way I was raising my son, with only my mother to turn to when I needed advice.

But now, I was not alone any longer. I found God, as well as a community of people who would come to my rescue if I so needed. I was encouraged to "live and depend on God," and that's just what I've been doing ever since. It was like a huge weight had been lifted off my shoulders, helping me carry the significant role of being the main role model in a young boy's life.

My faith served me well, and I discovered early on how I would not have coped without it. Because around the same period, when Marquise was in the sixth grade, my nephew Dewayne was engaging in a life of crime with gangs who were stirring up trouble in another state. In Dothan, Alabama, Dewayne's life would take a different turn.

VI

A LITTLE BIT OF SUNSHINE AND THEN THE DARKNESS

In the late 1980s and early 1990s, my nephew and Marquise joined the Sunshine Band Group under the affectionate tutelage of my then neighbor, Mrs. Virgie Chancellor. The lady is deceased now, but I am still in contact with her children. Our sons, in fact, were raised together. The band would travel from one nursing home to another performing their tunes; and this way, my son, my nephew, and other neighborhood kids would stay off the streets—doing something constructive.

Mrs. Chancellor would host Bible study sessions, and the kids would make costumes and act out little plays written from the most important stories of the Bible. This was their brand of entertainment, which they dished out to a willing audience of senior citizens every Sunday. Thus, they would sing and perform these plays at the nursing home. Mrs. Chancellor was a missionary, and with all her dedication, her greatest charity consisted of her efforts in keeping the children away from the dangers that would otherwise befall them in a city.

However, there was a little trouble brewing in paradise. As time passed, my nephew drifted away from the Bible group scene and wanted to follow the "crowd." Marquise, on the other hand, was pretty much a homebody; and his favorite activity was playing Nintendo games. As long as I had a game in the house, I could be certain he would be inside. At the same time, my nephew began changing and keeping company with the wrong kind of people; and this, of course, created problems in my home.

Several times, I sent him back to spend time with his dad, hoping that their interaction would inject some discipline in the boy's life. The whole plan backfired. His rebellion, rather than muting, intensified to the point where he started missing school days and getting in trouble. I knew one thing: I did not want my son to follow in these twisted footsteps. While these events were unfolding, my family was encouraging Marquise to make wise choices and follow a better direction.

Sometimes, however, when you tell children things, you wonder whether they are listening to you at all or whether your words fly right over their heads. We later found out that my nephew was a much greater influence than we had hoped he would be on my son. Dewayne was gravitating toward a negative lifestyle and Marquise was definitely taking notes—something we had done our best to avoid. But life always takes wild turns, and we often end up dealing with things we would rather not face. At this time, Marquise had not yet entered the double digits in age.

I did not fully realize that there was a problem, let alone the extent of it, until I confronted him about something he was doing and he responded with, "Ma, you do not have to worry." Something about the way he spoke put me on alert. But this time, as always, I let him speak and say his piece.

He said to me, "Ma, a while back, we were outside playing football and my uncle Aaron told me and Dewayne to stay focused and not be a follower but a leader. There are two ways to go in life, the right way or the wrong way." He paused for a second, took a deep breath, and continued, "Sometimes, I have gone the wrong way myself and wished I had an opportunity to start over again. I can't undo what I did, but I promise to have more patience when bad things come my way again. If you go the wrong way, you will be one of the statistics, if you choose the right way, you can be successful."

Marquise told me that Dewayne burst out laughing at him and then walked away. But he went on to say, "Uncle Aaron said to me, 'Dewayne thinks I am joking, but he is going to find out the truth later on in life.' He told me to just watch and see."

I observed my son as he watched his cousin in the years that passed. I saw him wake up to the realization that his uncle Aaron's words were prophetic. He made sure to keep company with people who were positive. Marquise and Dewayne had their own separate friends.

To make a long story short, my nephew immersed himself so deeply in his negative lifestyle that he was finally incarcerated in Alabama for six years to pay for crimes he had committed. It took a drastic series of events to prompt Dewayne to openly appreciate Marquise's decision to live life positively and choose the right path. He knew that Marquise had made new friends, built a new life without his cousin. Two of his greatest and most trusted friends at the time were called David Watkins, an African American boy, and Thomas James Casey, a Caucasian boy. He enjoyed hanging out with them, and they called themselves "friends to the end." Even when he got drafted, they made it a point to meet and spend time playing their favorite games when Marquise visited home. He was the tallest of the lot, but also the youngest. Perhaps he liked the idea of having friends older than him, in a sense reminding him of how he saw Dewayne as an older brother. I recall he also had another friend, an African American, by the name of Tommie. I always managed to get confused about the two Tommie's.

Marquise's friends whom he met when he was 12 years old. He was the tallest of the lot and 3-4 years younger than they. They loved playing games together during his visits all the way to his death. Marquise was in the NFL when this photo was taken. David Watkins and Thomas "Tommie" James Casey— "FRIENDS TO THE END".

Once he was out too late, skipping his curfew, so I went out looking for him. I went to one Tommie's house, but he wasn't there. When he came home, I was angry and asked him where he had been. He laughed and said, "Ma, I was by white boy Tommie's house, not *that* Tommie!" Despite the fact that later in life Marquise would be branded by a certain attorney I had hired as "racist"—and this because Marquise had made it clear that he was not happy with his work—we all knew better than anyone that Marquise had nothing but love for everyone, no matter their race, color, or creed.

Dewayne told Marquise many times during his period of confinement how he wished he would have listened, and his life would have taken a completely different turn. But the harsh truth was that he didn't pay attention to all the lessons we, and life itself, had tried to teach him.

I asked Dewayne if he wanted me to include his story in this book and he let me know that he wanted the truth known. He has long since admitted to himself that his uncle was not telling any lies and it had always been up to him to decide how to live his life.

He would tell me, "I took the wrong direction, and Marquise took the right direction. I hope someone will learn my story and make better decisions."

After I moved out from the old neighborhood, I remember him remarking that he didn't think he'd make it to twenty-one years of age because of all the crime he had witnessed among adults. It was so sad that any young man could think that way or even have to see these things. But today, Dewayne is alive and well and invests much energy in taking care of his biological mother. His example truly showed me and Marquise how life, when we are at the edge of hope, turns back around and comes full circle.

Every night, we would hear news of double and triple murders on television. This just wasn't the way to live, but it was reality for Dewayne. The sad part was that he and Marquise were brought up together, yet they had such different outlooks on life. I realized that personality and attitude play a huge part in crafting one's fate. The old story about looking at a glass that is half empty or half full is very apt—Marquise and Dewayne are perfect examples of these contrasting philosophies about life.

Today, Dewayne is out of jail and working hard. He had to learn the hard way, but the most important thing is that he did learn. One cannot avoid a tornado that is heading full speed against one's house. As the structure topples down and the bits and pieces are carried away by the raging windstorm, the only thing that remains is one's inner voice, one's conscience, telling one what should and should not have been done to prepare for the worst. In the aftermath of tragic events, we have all learned to be wise.

The story of Marquise and Dewayne was like a tale of two brothers who each make entirely different choices—one takes the path to growth and the other embarks on a journey toward destruction. Before his arrest, Dewayne was visiting his biological mother in Alabama. He thought the rules at our house were too strict, so he decided to go and live with his mother for a while.

But the fierce windstorm followed him there, tearing his playhouse down for good. For some reason, he made the acquaintance of some really shady people and became involved in an armed robbery case. He was not arrested at the scene but was stopped on the streets three days later and arrested following a lead given through an accusatory statement provided by a witness.

This was happening at a time in my life when I was doing my utmost to keep crime out of our lives and our home. So here I was, having to deal with this predicament and forced to start a battle within the judicial system with a broken heart and limited funds. I was living in one state, and the crime was committed in another state. I was shattered because this was my own blood, my nephew and pretty much an adoptive brother to my son.

Dewayne was now facing over twenty years of jail time for armed robbery with no possibility of parole. Prior to this, he had no criminal record. He was locked up for about two years until the trial, and this greatly affected him on the mental level. Of course, my son, my brother, and I traveled regularly to visit with him. I wanted Marquise to see firsthand what the judicial system is like and how easy it is to become embroiled in the activities taking place on the dark side of the world and, eventually, to lose oneself in the vise of an unforgiving system.

On our first trip there, we all met with Dewayne's attorney, and she let us know that Dewayne had no other choice but to plead guilty to the crime because the police had all the evidence pinned down in this case. Dewayne kept insisting on the one hand that he did not participate in an armed robbery; but his attorney, on the other hand, was talking about twenty-five years of incarceration if no guilty plea was made.

I felt that all I could do was to start praying because I knew it would be devastating to have to watch my nephew sentenced to so much jail time. He was only thirteen to fourteen years old when all of this occurred and had no prior juvenile record. But Dewayne was hardheaded, and as he had already amply proved, he would not listen to his elders for anything in the world.

As for me, I would have rather seen him get some help and avoid incarceration than succumb to stubbornness and pride at a time when there was no place for such attitude. I knew more than anyone how much Dewayne had suffered in his life and the conflicts he had had to deal with. I could never condone his behavior, but I could understand where it was coming from. He had experienced myriad emotional problems prior to being placed in our custody, and I couldn't just let him face his fate without doing my utmost to help him.

Hence, my brother and I decided to take things a little further and conduct our own investigation while we were there. We gathered more information and made our way to the attorney's office to see what her defense would be on behalf of my nephew. All I could tell her was to have a care with Dewayne's defense and to remember that she also had children.

During that visit, I somberly told her, "What you do to someone else's child, it shall return unto you or your child or children. I don't see how you would be able to sleep at night if you are not able to give Dewayne the best defense possible."

She looked at me with a strange expression and let us know that she would do her best. There was no defense plan set up, merely the suggestion of making a guilty plea in a case that could otherwise result in a twenty-five-year sentence. My nephew refused to go along with that plea, and we stood behind him because he was family and he was also a little boy who had been influenced by someone older, someone with an evil heart.

When we arrived at the courtroom, we could cut the aura of racism with a knife.

My son said to me, "These people look like they hate black people. Did Martin Luther King make it through this area?"

Little did he know, Rev. King did not get this far. Montgomery was the closest he got to this place. I felt embarrassment and hurt when he asked this question because this was my hometown, the place where I grew up—and there was nothing I could say or do at this time to make things easier on my son. It felt like the worst betrayal. The jury was selected, and from my memory, I can say that only one or possibly two black people were on it.

We were all united in this moment of pain, anxiously awaiting the outcome of Dewayne's trial which would seal his fate. Things were not looking good. Perhaps Marquise was hit more than all of us by the sheer gravity of the situation. He felt like he was losing his brother, one of the few people he looked up to in his life.

So in the midst of all our trepidation, the trial finally began; and after one mere day of listening and witnessing the goings-on, I was literally sick to the stomach. They had no witness, no weapon, the victim could not identify my nephew, and the officers' testimony was so twisted and convoluted that the judge told them to get off the stand one by one.

The district attorney sounded like he had a personal agenda pushing some kind of revenge, and I was wondering what in the world was the matter with everybody. Marquise had a wake-up call to the sheer reality of human relations—the ugly side of the equation. To my astonishment, despite the lack of evidence, it appeared that Dewayne was treated as a "guilty" party all the same. While all this was going on, I watched Marquise's confusion and desperation grow with each passing minute.

The next day, we returned to the courtroom, and Dewayne's attorney did her job and brought forth her defense because she knew there was no hard evidence against the boy in this case. When all witnesses had been called and everyone had said their piece, it was time for the jury to retire and come up with the verdict. After an hour or so (yes, an hour) of deliberating, the jury came back with a guilty verdict; and then we had to wait on the sentencing, which was scheduled for the next day. It turned out that Dewayne was the recipient of a twenty-year sentence based on no evidence and convoluted testimony.

How could anybody understand such a phenomenon? Perhaps laws are truly made to be broken, as some say. I could have dealt with a reduced sentence, but this was too much to swallow, given the circumstances. To me, it was simply unacceptable.

I was totally distraught; and this case, if nothing else, opened my eyes to witnessing firsthand how black males are being railroaded through the judicial system. Thanks to my prior experience serving on the jury in New Orleans, I had a little insight on how the judicial system ought to work as far as a trial is concerned. One thing I knew for a fact was that if there is any reasonable doubt attached to a case, then the verdict should not be a guilty verdict. The result in this case would most likely be a lower sentence, or else the charge is dropped altogether.

Just before the trial was adjourned at the end of the first day, I remember the DA stating, "This will be the trial of the century," and sadly, he was absolutely right. Because in all my years, I had never witnessed a trial in which there was no evidence presented or where the victim could not identify the accuser; and still, the jury would come back with a guilty verdict. I was blown away.

Marquise was crushed and deeply affected by this, and I felt utterly powerless at not being able to bring back his cousin, his "big brother," to our home and return to our regular life. If I could have turned back the clock and stopped this from happening, I would have. This incident drove him to lose faith in the system. I could clearly see his disillusionment, and it broke my heart.

Our little family unit had taken a harsh blow, and we all wondered whether these people had any sort of conscience. What made it worse was this was occurring in the very same town where I was born. I was beyond comprehension—how could they convict Dewayne without proof? Did this vicious behavior stop them from sleeping at night? This was Marquise's first big loss to the system, and I prayed it would be the last. He kept repeating those fateful words that his uncle Aaron had told him a few years earlier—the very words which both boys had initially taken as a joke. Perhaps he truly understood now more so than ever that he did not want to fall into this type of trap and become a helpless victim.

I could not deny that my nephew had been up to stirring trouble and wasting time with the wrong crowd. I was sure he had done something wrong or mischievous and that he was lying to me about his role in the incident, but I could not for a second believe that he was involved in armed robbery. I fought for Dewayne until the end, and I finally was able to get him out on bond after they sentenced him to twenty years.

I called an attorney in that area to discuss the sentence, and he told me that in all his years of practicing law, he had never heard of such a thing as what had transpired. His opinion was that the judgment was completely wrong. Following my discussion with this lawyer, I wrote a letter to the district attorney and judge, requesting them to forward me the court papers and threatened to expose the story to *60 Minutes* or *20/20* for a thorough investigation into the matter. However, they never would release the papers to me. Rather, they let Dewayne out on bond, knowing that he had to return soon and fully expecting that he'd be locked away for two decades following the court's sentencing.

Things were bound to get worse.

While the case was pending, during the time Dewayne was released on bond, he got in trouble again—this time it was a car theft. He was finding it hard to be convinced of the fact he could be cleared of the charges, so he figured he might as well keep complicating things. I had reached the point where I was tired of fighting for him. I realized then that my nephew needed some quiet time to think, and I reluctantly admit that the years he spent in jail may have been what he needed to make the necessary change. He had passed a year and a half in jail before he was sentenced, and thinking back, I think it was just what he needed to wake up and see what his reality was—it was either change or keep going to jail.

In the end, although he was sentenced to twenty long years, Dewayne served six years of jail time; and today, as I stated earlier, he has been released. Dewayne, a young man whose life had been marred by stigma, was set free during Marquise's sophomore year at LSU. He admits he wished he would have listened, and he is so glad that his cousin did not follow in his footsteps.

From that day forward, my son received a few lessons of life: avoid the wrong crowds, don't be a follower but a leader, and finally, if you see that trouble is on its way toward you, do not hesitate to start running away from it. Parents should repeatedly tell these things to their children, but sometimes one wonders if the little ones actually understand the implications of these teachings. I suppose that there is no guarantee, but it is still a duty that must be performed. I wanted my nephew to get something out of this so he could learn a valuable lesson. I also desperately wanted to make sure that I was getting the point across to Marquise. I hoped the events that befell us would speak for themselves, but I could not be sure that mere observation would be enough.

In any case, getting twenty years with no evidence was not the way I imagined it would be for Dewayne to learn his personal lesson. I knew my nephew was not an angel, and I also knew he should have known better than to participate in actions that would have involved him in theft and armed robbery. I strongly believe in the tenet that "if you do the crime, then you do the time." However, I also believe in a fair justice system, and I have always encouraged Marquise to share in my views. Sadly, in this case, justice had taken a holiday to a faraway, forgotten place.

I thought of our neighborhood and our children and how nobody seemed to care about rehabilitating our communities. Between 1991 and 1995, the murder rate in our city went up to four hundred a year or over, a fact my son had been exposed to most of his life. Perhaps because of this, Marquise decided at an early age that he did not want to be indifferent to what was going on around him. He wanted to be the one to fight injustice. He thought that some people got off the hook because they could buy themselves some justice, but others were not so lucky and wouldn't be given a fair hearing.

He wanted to share his experiences, beliefs, and thoughts with others, especially children, so they could take note and learn from them. I think that perhaps he was born to help others this way. The willingness to do things for others literally shone through in everything that he did. Such energy he had!

So despite his undesirable experience in the second grade and his further negative experiences with the "establishment" later on in life, this did not deter him from visiting the school years later as an adult—particularly when he was in college and then when he was part of the NFL. He told me all the time that he wanted to do it for the children. One bad experience, he felt, would not have justified him denying the children a privilege that he had so desired for himself when he was their age.

He wanted to spend time with these children, talk to them, and treat them with dignity. Looking at their fresh young faces was to him like looking into a mirror. Perhaps being with them reminded him of the hurt he had experienced at the abandonment from his father. He wanted to embrace them all and let them know they were not alone in this cold, unforgiving world. That someone cared for them in some measure, even if they thought they were alone.

He signed autographs, listened to them, gave them his undivided attention, and told them about the importance of pursuing a good education. He told them things a father would. The thing these young boys and girls needed most was someone to truly listen and understand their dreams and aspirations—someone to shine a light on the right path and guide them through it.

I remember when he went there, he stayed with them for about three hours; and before going, he told me, "Ma, I am not going to deny the children the opportunity I longed for when I was a child. I know that God will bless me because of what happened to me."

This is precisely the sort of thing that filled his heart with joy.

VII

A NEW ROUTE TO AVOID THE STREETS OF NEW ORLEANS

After graduation from the fifth grade, my son thought he was ready for a change, to move to a different school, because of all the problems in our community brought about by territorial gangs. He never wanted to catch the bus to school, and he knew that if he was caught in an area that others felt he did not belong to, then he could have possibly been attacked or even killed without so much as a reason. My nephew Dewayne was also aware of the seriousness of the situation, and despite his own personal problems or perhaps because of them, he would advise Marquise to stay off the streets.

Children of the 1980s and 1990s were faced with all kinds of challenges, and they knew the true face of evil while growing up in tough neighborhoods. They saw the parents of their classmates walking the streets at night, high on some drug or other, mostly crack cocaine. A "crackhead" would normally end up renting or giving up his or her car to a drug dealer in exchange for crack cocaine, and this particular act was generally referred to in our world as a "rock rental."

I told my son one day, "As long as you don't see me on the corner prostituting or doing drugs but you see me each day trying to make an honest living, you better do what you are supposed to do in school and be somebody so you can take care of yourself. I feel that you and I deserve good grades when the report cards come out. I work too hard for you to come home with Cs and Ds."

So keeping all this in mind, by the time fifth grade knocked on Marquise's door, I had already moved out of that area where I had rented my first apartment. This was his first year at a new school, the Bishop Perry Middle School; and for some reason or other, he could never adjust to this new environment. In the first place, the school was located in another section of the city, different from the one he was used to. Secondly, his love for sport and his ambitions to grow as an athlete were starting to shine through and that desire in itself sparked further changes in his outlook on life. Thirdly, he had experienced the "cursing" incident at this institution.

He never seemed at ease at this particular school, and most especially, he had no way of indulging his love of sport too seriously while he stayed there. So after the sixth grade, I was faced with making yet another change and placed him in Fannie C. Williams Middle School. It was while he was there that he began to participate in tag football and basketball. The school was much closer to home and to the places he was familiar with. There, he was able to see most of his old friends, and I could tell that he was much more comfortable this time around.

During this period, he began having growth spurts; and by eighth grade, he was six feet five, and his nickname at school was Baby Shaq. He would eventually grow to be six feet seven, and just under three hundred pounds—a gentle giant with a heart bigger than his body. I remember him coming home crying that year because the other children were teasing him. They laughed at his big feet and his excessive height. I was afraid he would succumb to bad behavior; and I made sure to keep him occupied with chores, training sessions, and study routines.

My brother Aaron also gave him a father-to-son talk and told him not to cry about that but rather to go back to school and tell his friends, "You see these big feet? That means money, and this height also means money, so all I have to do is to apply myself and keep my mind focused and my grades up—I will do anything I can do not to be an empty head when I graduate."

My brother went on to tell him that a love and an aptitude for sports can be both an advantage and a risk. You can reap great rewards, but you can also get hurt and lose everything. The best one can do is to apply oneself both mentally and physically. It was obvious early on that Marquise possessed both the size and the ability to pursue an athletic career. Yet he had to always keep in his mind not to put all his eggs in one basket. He had to learn to grasp opportunity as it came and to make the most of it while at the same time developing his intellect on different levels.

This stage of Marquise's life marked the onslaught of adolescence, that part of a child's life when the parent must work extra hard to ensure their offspring's protection and education. It is important to make particularly sure that learning becomes an integral part of a child's life, and teaching is a gift never to be discounted or dismissed. I requested reports from his teachers and nannies with respect to his progress. Luckily for all of us, I never had to deal with Marquise having drug problems and ruining his life in that manner. In this particular regard, he had always been a good child.

However, I still kept an eye out for him and watched as closely as possible. I wanted to see what kind of company he kept—good or bad—and I also had to personally ensure that Marquise would always choose to be a leader, not a follower. I knew I had to put my foot down and make no allowances in this regard.

To this end, I created "behavior slips" each day. The slip was to be his ever-present companion, just like his book bag. It would leave with him in the morning and come back home with him in the evening. The important part was that it had to be filled out and signed by his teachers each and every day. On any given day, they would note not only his behavior but also his attentiveness in class and the acceptability of his homework.

Basically, I would have a specially tailored daily report. The teachers were great and always willing to cooperate with me. I specially designed this paper slip so that my son would not be able to take it upon himself to alter it on his own. In the days on which I did not get a completed slip, I assumed that there was a problem.

The teachers told me that, thanks to my idea, his behavior in class changed a lot and for the better. He had never been unruly, but this type of loving discipline kept him firmly in line. If something didn't add up on the written report, I would automatically go the school to find out what was going on. Marquise knew that I was prepared to take off from work to deal with some nonsense, and he also knew I would not be very happy about that. It was woe unto him, and I had to be consistent. I could not miss a beat at all. At one point, my son was convinced I was crazy and that I was ready to set him straight at any time if his behavior got out of line. In essence, my plan worked splendidly.

VIII

LOOKING FOR STARDOM

Marquise was highly recognized by many coaches from different schools during his eighth-grade year. They saw the potential in this boy. After his graduation from Fannie C., he wanted to attend a school with a good football and academic program; so after some rather disastrous tentative choices, he finally decided to go to DeLaSalle. It was here that his talent burst to the fore and took everyone by storm.

Marquise's sophomore year at DeLaSalle High School.
My son, Antonio, Bocchus and Coach Leaumont

Prior to making his decision to attend DeLaSalle, his sojourn at another school turned out to be quite unpleasant. He felt he was being treated like a dummy—his athletic prowess developed and his academic efforts summarily ignored, and that was not acceptable to him. After drumming into his head the importance of getting an exemplary education, he felt he would be missing out by attending a school which cared none for his mental skills.

It was so bad that one time, he was placed in the back of the classroom with a book and told not to worry about academics. Then and there, he refused that offer point-blank, saying he was not going to be an empty-headed dummy. That same day, he called his grandmother to come and pick him up so he could register for ninth grade at another school, which happened to be DeLaSalle.

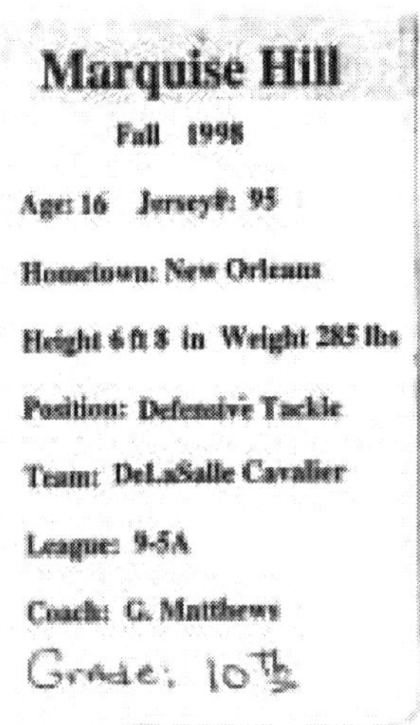

Marquise's first trading card.

Marquise's last high school trading card that I hired a Photographer to make. You can locate and purchase LSU and NFL trading cards on Various Website.

At this point, I began to see the maturity burgeoning inside him. He liked the academic structure and sports program at the new school, and he blossomed under the tutelage of the wonderful teachers and coaches there. He participated in basketball and track, as well as football—but the latter was his love. His dedicated coach helped mold him and instill in him the desire to work hard. My mother and I wore out two sets of tires a year for four years, taking him back and forth to school so he would never miss training, but there is no doubt in my heart and mind that it was worth it. For it was at this school that he first started garnering media attention and thus earned recognition as one of the most talented defensive linesmen in the United States.

Marquise really enjoyed attending the DeLaSalle School. He had to work hard in the classroom and play hard on the field, which was a challenge for him. The football season at the school gave him his first taste of glory. However, there was one problem—the fact that Marquise was a bad loser. He was often hard on himself when he made mistakes. Nonetheless, he always respected teams that beat their opponents honestly. If he saw any cheating going on during the game, he would never fail to let it be known to the referee coach. He had a low tolerance for dishonest practices, both on and off the field.

I believe that most sports, but particularly football, were etched into his DNA. He worked hard all the time to become a better player, and his enthusiasm was contagious. The fever caught everybody around him, including me. Marquise was intensely focused on his commitments and did all he could to avoid trouble. As would have been expected, he never wanted to catch the bus because of the incidence of high crime in our neighborhood. His greatest fear was being dragged into a fight and getting in trouble with the law. Dewayne's case had made a terrible mark on him, but I have to admit it was probably best this way because it kept him safe from the streets.

The distance from my house to the school was approximately fifteen miles one way; and we made many trips, sometimes two to three trips a day, to get him to the classroom. Unfortunately at the time, there was no direct bus service to the school, so we had no choice but to drive.

We were making so many trips to the school that one time I expressed my anger to the coach for making our children train so often and have them go to the school at unreasonable hours. Lo and behold, I found out that it was my son who wanted to execute these trips for his own personal reasons, and they had nothing to do with the demands of the coach. He requested the keys to the locker room so he could work out before school opened every morning, sometimes as early as five or six o'clock in the morning. He would then take a shower, change his clothes and go to class. Then again, he would work out and practice in the evening. I had to apologize to his coach for jumping to conclusions.

I knew one thing: by the end of the year, my car had gone through the wringer. However, I also confirmed another thing: Marquise's routine never failed, and day after day, he demonstrated great discipline. A discipline mostly unparalleled by any other boy of his age. How could I be upset with him for wanting to work so hard?

For four years, we traveled back and forth uptown to the classic neighborhood with the streetcar running down the middle of the streets. This was the New Orleans most people see when they tour the Big Easy. Tourists would see a charming sleepy neighborhood with pretty parks of rolling green, lush foliage, gorgeous gardens, and imposing mansions.

This was not the New Orleans we lived in, but that did not stop Marquise from dreaming.

He would always tell me, "You know what, Ma? One day I want to live up here to see what it is like. I know it will take a lot of hard work and a good job to live on this street."

I never crushed his aspirations and goals because I knew Marquise was capable of doing great things in his life. And he did. I just wish he had had more time.

By attending DeLaSalle, he was able to see kids and parents who had more money than they could handle, although some friends did not have love in their home. Even there, he met many teens his age who were not happy at home. So he was able to look into both worlds and see how blessed he really was because he was cherished and loved. His Big Mom, mom, and uncles worked hard to surround him with stability and let him know he could be whatever he wanted to be.

By this time, we had moved away from the old neighborhood, away from the crime that destroyed the area like a festering wound. I had moved out of our first apartment during Marquise's fifth-grade year. But it seemed that crime and problems would follow us wherever we went, and we still had to face more problems in the new neighborhood. Hence, this was the reason for me needing to drive my son back and forth from school rather than allow him to weave through the jungle on his own.

While attending DeLaSalle, he became really close to the administrators, especially Mrs. Gelpi. They were wonderful people who loved Marquise to death and treated him like he was a little treasure. He would always tell me, "Ma, did you know I had a white mom and dad?" referring to Mr. and Mrs. Gelpi. During his years there, they were indeed his parents away from home.

Marquise on the court playing basketball (#55). Marquise played basketball, football and ran track while at DeLaSalle High School; he received offers for basketball scholarships as well.

In the meantime, while he built bonds in his new school, he played basketball and track during his freshman, sophomore, and junior years. During his final year, he wanted to concentrate on football, the sport of his heart. By his junior year, he was almost on every college list in America, labeled as an All-American, his feats on the field lauded in countless national sports publications. He played hard and worked hard. He was determined not to let anything stop him from reaching his goal.

One of his teachers was Ms. Calder. I was talking to her recently, in March of this year (a year after my son's death), during the ceremony when Marquise was inducted in the Hall of Fame in New Orleans. She told a story of when one time, Marquise was out of his seat in class and she told him, "Marquise, go back to your seat, or I'll knock your knees off!" At that point, another student interrupted and said to Marquise, "Are you going to let Ms. Calder talk to you like that?" Marquise replied sarcastically, "Definitely so, I will take my seat because I need my knees to play in the NFL!" When she finished her story, we all laughed about it. I thought it was a great, moving story coming from one of Marquise's teachers.

But let me go back to his days in DeLaSalle. He was so determined because he saw a lot of his friends die on the streets or get incarcerated, so he was adamant not to fall in that mousetrap and be at the mercy of the system. One day, one of his close friends was shot in the head while playing a game. It was a terrible tragedy—another event that affected him profoundly.

We kept up with the news, staying posted on the murder rate in New Orleans, which rose to a new high every day. So knowing all this, Marquise always played his games and stayed inside so he would not get caught up with all of the bad things that were going on in the world around the bubble of his life.

Respect the less fortunate, handicapped, homeless, and elderly. That is the message my mother made sure to drum into him. The elderly deserve respect because they know the way in life. Race, color, or creed are incidental and do not matter. This belief was ingrained in him early on in life.

One time Marquise told me about a story his uncle had told him when he was but a small boy.

It went something like this: One time an old gentleman met a young man and advised him not to turn around the next corner. Every day, however, the young man passed that corner and turned, ignoring the old man's advice. Each day he would also see the old man sitting in the same spot, doling out the same advice to every person in sight. So after relating this story, my brother asked my son, "What if you came across an old man and he told you not to go around that corner? What would you do? Heed the man, or go around that corner?" The correct answer would be: heed the old man because the old man has been sitting there for a long time and he has watched all the traffic that's been going around that corner. The old man knows that around the corner lies trouble and possibly death.

The moral of the story is that older people have accumulated a lot of information in their lives, and we have to take our time and listen. As my mother would always say to me, "You must go where I have been, keep on living, and you will see."

Around his senior year at DeLaSalle, my son had received over a hundred letters from different schools both small and large. He was confident that his dream could become reality if he kept his mind focused and let no one and nothing distract him. I could clearly see that he really enjoyed the attention, but at the same time, he always wanted to stay humble. It was like he was subject to two conflicting forces where one would allow the other to surface, depending on the situation.

He often told me, "Ma, I do not want my head to swell so much that I walk through the door and snub a little child or handicapped person who wants me to greet them or sign an autograph."

He was fully cognizant and understanding of the fact that something small like that can make a difference in a person's life. He felt that if he could make a difference and make someone happy, he did not want to deny anyone anything.

I began collecting the letters from colleges as he was receiving them. I had a six boxes of them sitting in a box in our garage. Unfortunately, years later, we lost all of them in the Katrina disaster. His plan had been to make a collage out of them. He was incredibly sad to discover that we had lost so many pictures and memories in the aftermath of the hurricane.

In the year 2000, the summer prior to my son's senior year in high school, he took his first official job at Jazzland. This turned out to be one good life lesson. I always stressed the importance of getting a good education, and this was one of those instances when the teaching hit home.

I often told him that nobody wants to be working at a job one detests or does not want. However, sometimes these experiences are necessary in our quest to prepare ourselves for the real world, as living on this earth is not an easy task to accomplish.

Marquise had his feet planted firmly on the ground. He knew early on that he enjoyed football, but he also made sure to remember that such a career would not last forever; and unfortunately, like so many other jobs in this world, it is not guaranteed. The only thing guaranteed was his knowledge and education in both academics and sports—those were things nobody could take away from him. Football could bring either untold success on the one hand or disappointments, pain, and permanent injury on the other hand.

I instilled in his mind that, whatever he did, he always needed to have a plan A and a plan B. I never failed to demonstrate to him that I would always hope and pray for him to reach his goal, but if something occurred and he did not, I would never ever be disappointed by him. I was proud of him no matter the outcome. All I wanted him to do was to complete school and be successful and happy, whether in a football career or otherwise.

So with all my lessons brewing in his mind, Marquise took his first job. At the end of the first day of work at Jazzland, I picked him up; and when I saw his face, I knew I would never forget that day. Sometimes the memory comes to the fore, and it still has the power to make me chuckle. When I arrived at the location, he was standing outside waiting on me. He had taken his shirt off. I noticed a frown on his face and a pout on his lips. At first, I thought he might have been fighting or had gotten in some sort of scrape, but I couldn't fathom what that could be. And then, he was not the fighting kind unless he was faced with extreme circumstances, such as the time he had been run over by a car while riding his bike.

I do recall that it was about ninety-nine degrees out there that day. He was huffing and puffing, although most of that was not owing to the temperature.

When he got into the car, he turned to me immediately and said, "Hey Ma . . ."

"Yes?" I replied, trying hard not to smile at the fractious expression on his face.

His words rolled from his tongue like a waterfall. "I quit. I feel like I have been working in a field like a slave. Just from the outside looking in, it looks like minority people were doing all of the hard work and certain ones of the same age were doing easy work and I feel that's unfair."

He paused to take a breath and then said to me, "You know what, Ma? You won't ever have to worry about your son getting a good education. Trust me, I am going to get my education because I can see why you have always taught me to learn all I can learn. Because in the real world life is not fair."

I let him speak without interruption, but after he was finished, I did point out that he could not just quit a job. There were too many things he wanted, such as a car, for instance; and he had the responsibility to take care of those things. After watching his forlorn expression, I felt my heart constricting. I knew he would not have quit if it wasn't that bad. Marquise was never one to shun hard work and avoid his responsibilities.

As soon as he had obtained this job, my brother, who lived in Alabama, had made arrangements to get his old car fixed up for him. Marquise used some of his summer money to get repairs done to it, and my brother picked up the remaining cost. We would not deny him that car. Soon thereafter, we made a trip up there to pick up the car, and my son drove it home. He was so very happy because he would have a car for his senior year in high school.

Unfortunately, his elation did not last very long. For my son's third game in high school, his team was playing their archrival, the St. Augustine team. When the game was over and the boys made their way back to their respective schools, Marquise found to his horror that someone had stolen his car.

He was already upset, thinking about how his team had lost the game. Now his car was gone. Marquise had installed a good sound system in it and that was really what the thieves had wanted as the car itself wasn't worth that much. Luckily, we found the car in an abandoned spot, almost three to four months later. Until we did, however, I felt compelled to sacrifice my comfort and let him drive my SUV to school because he was so disappointed. All of this occurred during the first part of the season.

IX

DOUBLE-CROSSED

I named this chapter thus because my son's favorite movie was called *Doublecrossed.* It starred a very capable Dennis Hopper in the lead role and was based on Barry Seal's death sentence in New Orleans. Barry Seal was a DEA informant who helped the US government take down the drug lords in South America. Rather than be acquitted or awarded a reduced sentence, however, he was "double-crossed," sentenced to death, and executed.

At an early age, Marquise was very much aware of the drug trafficking problem, especially in rough neighborhoods. He knew the numbers, and he also knew the consequences of choosing a wayward life. This movie gave him further insight into it—into the ways people get their hands dirty in this criminal life—and he was more determined than ever to stay out of trouble.

However, it seemed that trouble was often ready and willing to find *him*—not because he ever got into drugs (he never did) but for different reasons. Unfortunately, it was his destiny to become double-crossed by the justice system and an attorney I hired in the same instance. He was reliving his favorite movie, only in a different role and in altogether different circumstances—perhaps not as dramatic as in Barry Seal's case, but disillusioning nonetheless.

Prior to his death this year, Marquise had just looked up this movie and purchased a copy because it had had such an impact on his thinking—he had already owned a copy; but like so many other things, it was lost in the hurricane. One may ask, what does a movie about drug lords and dirty deals have to do with Marquise Hill? The answer is that I felt that mention of Marquise's favorite movie seemed like an apt introduction to a chapter which discusses some more tough challenges that Marquise had to face in his short but meaningful life. In the following paragraphs, you will see the reason why.

Marquise's last year at DeLaSalle was a turning point in his life. While on his way to a track meet at another school in the same area, he was confronted with something he had never experienced before in life. This episode became a lesson of life—one he would surely never have forgotten—had he lived to be a hundred years old. It affected my son dearly, and he was determined that he would never let this happen to him again. Sometimes, however, will alone is not enough to keep pain and disappointment at bay.

Prior to this incident, my son was telling me about certain school teams they were playing against and that he was encountering problems with certain players. His efforts were therefore directed at avoiding them as much as possible. However, when it was time for the track meet, all of those schools came together for this event and there was no way he could avoid a confrontation. Those same players Marquise had told me about were all present—and ready to start something bad.

On this particular day, on March 16, 2000, the students traveled to the track meet, to be held at Chalmette, by bus. When my son and his classmates arrived at the stadium, he and his classmates were confronted by students from another school (as is usually the case with these sort of events, many schools were involved in this particular meet).

As misfortune would have it, as they alighted the bus, a group of Caucasian students started calling them "niggers" and kept pushing the N-word around. My son approached the main individual who had instigated the controversy (and who, for the purposes of this book, shall be named Jeremy Lincoln) and told him he was not there to make any trouble but to participate in the track meet.

He asked the boy one question, "Why are you acting this way?"

Marquise and his team turned and walked away. At my son's words, most of the boys in the other group also turned and walked away. However, the young man who had initiated this incident turned all of a sudden and called to his friends to follow him.

"Don't you walk away from me!" he shouted, once again qualifying his tirade with the N-word.

Marquise did not want a fight. He was trying to maintain a positive attitude and stay away from anything that could put him in difficulty or danger. This would have been one of those situations, but it was hard to avoid a scene with all these boys confronting him and his teammates.

"What are you trying to do? Are you trying to get something started?" my son told the other boy.

Immediately, Marquise turned his back to him, again, and walked off.

The boy, rearing for a fight, rushed to him and hit Marquise in the back of the head; and he, in turn, hit him back. He had no choice but to defend himself.

So as all this was going on, the boy's dad came over and started shouting at Marquise's team, "All you niggers are going to jail!"

He kept saying this over and over like a litany. Subsequently, my son was handcuffed, placed in a police car, and taken to juvenile detention. He had never been in a police car or arrested for anything prior to this day. Of course, this is just the type of thing I was praying would not ever happen to him; and surely, I would never have thought such incidents could happen at a track meet of all places!

Someone contacted me at work and told me that Marquise was being detained by the police. As anyone could imagine, for me to say that I was nervous and upset would be an understatement. I know what my son was capable of and how strong he was; but I also knew that if he was in a fight, gentle as he was, something must surely have caused it—and that something could not have been him. Marquise was patient and calm, but he had a threshold that nobody should have crossed, or there would be problems. Like so many of us, he had his limitations, and obviously that threshold had been crossed most definitely in this case.

I have always told him he was too big to pick fights and to never be the one to start a fight. He knew this and respected this. Never before this unfortunate event had he started a fight, with or without provocation, so I knew better than to believe he had made an exception this time. Whatever he had done, it was justified. I just had to learn the details.

I went to the police station and spoke to my son. I believed everything he told me. I told Marquise that I would head to the stadium immediately, while people were still at the track meet, to look into the matter. Surely someone had seen what had transpired.

When I arrived there, a man walked up to me and asked me if I was Marquise's mother.

"Yes," I replied.

"Ms. Hill," the man said, "your son was only defending himself, and he did nothing wrong. The other person was in the wrong because I saw the entire thing. Get yourself a good lawyer. I can't be involved because I may get in trouble for saying this, but I wanted you to know anyway."

"I understand, sir. Thank you for telling me this," was my response.

This man had approached me near the parking lot outside the facility. He did not want to be involved in any ensuing dispute, and therefore, he never told me his name. This, however, was not the end of it. An anonymous caller—a witness—called Marquise's school and stated that the student in question had made it a habit to start fights and bother other students and had been suspended from the school because of this incident. Every official I spoke to admitted that this incident had been handled very badly, and the other boy's bad reputation preceded him everywhere.

With the exception of the incident in 5th grade, from the time he was in kindergarten to the twelfth grade, Marquise had never been in a school fight, nor was there a record of him fighting anywhere outside of school. Marquise was not a problem child, plain and simple.

So why had my boy been arrested?

This was a question I asked so many times, it must be etched in my brain. I never received a clear answer, except to realize the extent to which justice can be thwarted at the hands of the wrong people.

Subsequently, the bond was processed, and my son was released. At a later date, he was charged with a felony. The rationale for this remains a mystery to me. Even the judge did not see a reason for it. Eventually, the felony charge was reduced to simple battery. All this happened when my son was seventeen, and they waited until he had turned eighteen to go to court so that I would not have any say so in the matter, at least not legally. To add insult to injury, all of Marquise's witnesses had not received their subpoenas—and I found this to be very strange indeed. The picture started taking shape, but not in the way I had envisioned. At the end, the fact remained that my son had been arrested simply for defending himself.

Unfortunately, the attorney I hired (who in this book shall be named Mr. Garrett) was in cahoots with the DA; and rather than do his duty to protect my son, he turned the barrel on me, taking my money and convincing my son to agree to a reprehensible plea bargain. It was bad enough for a single parent to be facing the challenge of trying to keep their child out of the prison system, but it is even worse when you hire an attorney and pay them with your hard-earned money and they sell you out without even having the decency of informing you of what is going on.

I kept inquiring about my son's case, and the lawyer told everyone not to worry and that everything was in place. He continued taking my money, and I kept calling him for updates, which he never provided. I thought that, surely, he would eventually tell me we have resolved this matter and that the case was thrown out. My lawyer persisted in feeding me lies, and all the while, I was under the mistaken impression that everything was under control. So I was fighting two fights—one to protect my son and the other to get my attorney to cooperate. I could not just up and fire my attorney because I had already paid this one so much money that I was financially drained.

How much can a person take? Your child is attacked, placed in a police car, and charged with a felony in court; and the attorney you hired turns a knife in your back at the same time. My blood pressure went straight up. This unfortunate incident affected my son tremendously; but luckily, rather than rile out and react negatively, he began releasing his anxiety and stress in the weight room and out on the field. I, on the other hand, did not have a field to go to, no game to play, no gym; and there was nothing I could do but pray to the man up stairs to show me the way.

But the way things were going, I was wondering if God had tired of me asking him for help. This was the point when my son's five or six witnesses waited for a subpoena that never came. The lawyer did not legally represent me but Marquise; so in a desperate effort to acquire some semblance of control, I wrote to the Disciplinary Counsel, the NAACP, and everyone under the sun, asking for assistance. At the end, no one would come forward to help me; I was pretty much fighting a losing battle by myself.

To this day, I have all the documentation relating to this case. The paperwork went through the storm, but it is still readable. I remember the hearing where they have to determine if the person will be charged with a certain felony or simple battery. In my son's case, as you already know, it was a felony at first; then, it was reduced to simple battery. My lawyer told me I did not have to show up for this hearing and that everything was supposed to be copasetic.

From day one, I wanted a trial and was told by another attorney that it would be best to get an attorney who is actually experienced in legal matters in that area rather than an outsider. In light of this advice, I had decided to hire an attorney in the Orleans Parish area. This same attorney told me later that my son would be charged with simple battery rather than a felony—obviously, an outright lie.

Wanting to have more control over the situation, I did my own research. Another attorney informed me of the fact that my son could only have been charged with a felony if an object—a weapon—was used. Thank God, there was no weapon. So I said to myself, *Once we go to trial, that's when the truth will come out.* My lawyer told me we were going to trial from day one, which is really what I wanted. In a courtroom, Marquise would be able to call witnesses and have the opportunity of defending himself. That would be the best he could ever ask for. My financial constraints were great, but getting my son out of this fix was a priority. Nothing else mattered.

The really bad news came when I showed up in court because I realized how naïve I had been to trust my attorney. The court date was set at six months after the incident, and by this time, Marquise had reached the age of eighteen years. When the time came to begin selecting the jury, my lawyer came to tell me, "It would be best for your son to plead guilty to simple battery."

Upon hearing those dreaded words, it felt like my lungs had imploded, and I lost my composure then and there.

Unfazed, he continued by facetiously saying, "Come to think of it, your son is eighteen now, and he will have to make the decision himself. I will talk to him."

I knew his game was to strip me of my power and present a picture to my son whereby he'd be sure Marquise would agree to whatever he was suggesting. He was, after all, a lawyer; and he had, like many other lawyers, the gift of gab. He wouldn't have to work hard to get what he wanted.

To cut a long story short, he gave my son two choices: if he went to trial, he would risk being convicted on a much worse charge (a felony charge) and lose his scholarships; if he did not, he could plead guilty to simple battery and he would be able to turn a fresh page and move on.

I was angry, hurt, and thoroughly distressed. I broke apart right there in the courtroom because I knew this would leave the door open for a new can of worms—my son being the brunt of a civil suit following a guilty plea. I knew this from my research, so I tried telling my son not to listen to the attorney and not to take the plea. Being eighteen, he did not know much about how these things worked and the implications of his actions.

Marquise, however, was terrified of losing his scholarships. The attorney knew that nothing in the world meant more to Marquise than getting one of those scholarships, and he ruthlessly played on that fear. I knew better, but despite my knowledge, I could not get Marquise to understand the dynamics of the situation.

All he would say to me was, "Ma, don't worry about that. Those people will pay for their wrongdoing one day."

So Marquise took a guilty plea. In the end, the DA walked over to him and said, "Shake my hand, boy"—knowing full well that his words would prove an echo to long past slavery days. Marquise ignored him and walked past him, leaving the man behind with his hand extended into space.

Needless to say, I was livid, shaken by the entire incident. I took off from my job and drove fifteen miles to the attorney's office to let him know that I had no money to pay all the court costs. When he offered to loan me the money, that was the moment in which I completely lost it. I told him that I did not appreciate his underhanded treatment of both my son and me. In no uncertain terms, I told him that I did not like how he had handled this case. I was determined to pull my son out of school, and I wanted to go to the media and give them the entire story. I am not sure if I had ever felt so upset in my life, even during the time when Dewayne was in trouble.

I had to see a doctor because of my skyrocketing blood pressure and stress. My life and health were on the line. I had to calm myself down and started a habit of making myself count to ten before acting or talking. I wanted those people to pay for what they did. I wanted to expose my attorney and his so-called professionalism and integrity. I was angry with the entire world, the entire system.

Finally, I came to my senses and started thinking about my son's athletic career, which was a gift I wanted to protect and not destroy. I felt that the school should have been held responsible because their duty was to ensure that our children were looked after and nothing like this would happen to them. The attorney should have been held accountable for the role he played in carelessly representing my son. At the end of it all, it was me and

Marquise against the financial and social giants of this world because, no matter how much we screamed for help, nobody had come to our rescue, including those people and organizations which pride themselves with helping to resolve these situations.

Another thing worth mentioning is that during this time, I worked with the police department, so I had access to the MONA System documents. After retrieving the necessary information, I found out that a warrant had been issued for my son's arrest following my noncooperation with the way my lawyer handled the charges. Although the court had dropped the charges and substituted simple battery, somehow I discovered that the felony charge was in the system.

The reality of the situation was that I protested when Marquise was required to do community service because I did not like the fact that they wanted him to perform this task on the open roads or highways. All I could think of was that he could get hit or shot at while working; anything can happen when one is so exposed to all kinds of danger. This was another source of anxiety for me, but Marquise, always so strong and dutiful, took it in stride.

So I requested through the courts that Marquise be asked to perform his community service at the juvenile division where I worked—which is what he thankfully was allowed to do. By the time the storm was over, Marquise and I were both also hit with a $50,000 civil lawsuit; and finally, Marquise was made to pay $10,000 in a settlement. This, he covered dutifully, albeit not without resentment. I made my objections clear and said I would have gone to jail before paying a cent.

Three years later, the simple battery charge was still on his record. He wondered about Dr. Martin Luther King's struggles and felt that the world had still so much to learn from this great man. He thought it very important to address anything that was unfair or unjust in all facets of his life—including school. He started seeing life through a whole new pair of lenses.

DeLaSalle reprimanded Marquise for this incident, and they informed him that his behavior went against the school policy, which in some ways was to be expected. Although they did investigate, theirs was a zero-tolerance policy with respect to fighting. My son understood the consequences of his actions, yet he felt he was racially attacked and another victim of racism. Consequently, as a result of this, he also felt he had a right to defend himself. He disagreed with the school's actions toward him, but he did not make this a bigger deal than it already was, and he accepted the suspension with equanimity.

Apart from all the other outside evidence and testimony, an anonymous phone call was also made to the school to let the administration know that their student (i.e., my son) did not initiate the fight, but the school never acted on that call to investigate the matter in depth—although they said they had. Marquise was on his own this time.

The following letter was written by Marquise and sent to the Louisiana Attorney Disciplinary Board. It is in response to the lackluster and in crucial moments, it appeared, the absent defense made in court by our attorney during the case discussed in this chapter. Marquise here mentions how the attorney, whom I paid to defend him, "switched sides" and engaged in unethical behavior. The letter has been edited for clarity and the names of third parties have been omitted or changed. The names Mr. Garrett and Jeremy Lincoln are fictitious. They have been changed to protect the privacy of those involved. Marquise's signature is scanned and inserted below.

Louisiana Attorney Disciplinary Board
Office of the Disciplinary Counsel
4000 S Sherwood Forest Blvd. Suite 607
Baton Rouge, LA 70816

Marquise Hill
P. O. Box XXXXX
Baton, Rouge, LA 70893

Complaint No# 0013892

Attn: XXXXXX

Date: 11-8-01

Dear XXXXXX,

My mother informed me of the letter she received from your office. She read the letter to me and I couldn't believe the things Mr. Garrett was saying. I witnessed him telling my mother he was going over to St. Bernard and file.

I have worked with all types of people: white, black, yellow and red. I am not a racist and my mother isn't either. The reason we did not want to file charges was because we knew some people were stuck in time and still living in the day before I was born and they are very sick people.

I am a huge guy and I do not go around picking fights with people and calling them racist names. This is what happened to me. My mother taught me better than that. Jeremy Lincoln called me a 'nigger' and I turned my back and walked away. This is when he attacked me and I responded in self-defense. Why were they trying to charge me with a felony when we have many black men selling drugs and dying on our streets?

The real sick victims are the Lincoln family; Mr. Garrett and the Justice System if this matter can't be corrected. Mr. 'Justice of the Peace' Lincoln upholds his son in attacking people and calling them out of their name because of the color of their skin. Mr. Garrett completed college courses in Law and can't determine between Justice and Politics (personal gain); the justice system backs all of this up. Where is my role model and where's my justice?

My mother paid Mr. Garrett $1700.00 to prevent me from receiving a criminal record just for defending myself.

Mr. Garrett told me to get all of my witnesses in court because we were going to trial on Sept 26, 2000. Mr. Garrett never stated to me we were going for a guilty plea until we were in court. My witnesses wanted to know why they weren't called to testify. My mother was very upset about this in court. She requested another court date. Mr. Garrett was interested in getting a guilty plea. He just caught us off guard. He refused to get another trial date. My mother asked him at least five times about another court date. She also wanted to know why he switched his loyalty in the court room.

I was not really happy with this plea at all and will not allow this drama to stop me. I know for sure every dog has his day. I have to treat people right because I was taught that.

I can at least respect my mother because she believes in standing up for what's right regardless of color.

Sincerely,

#91

Marquise Hill
Keep your Eye on the Tiger

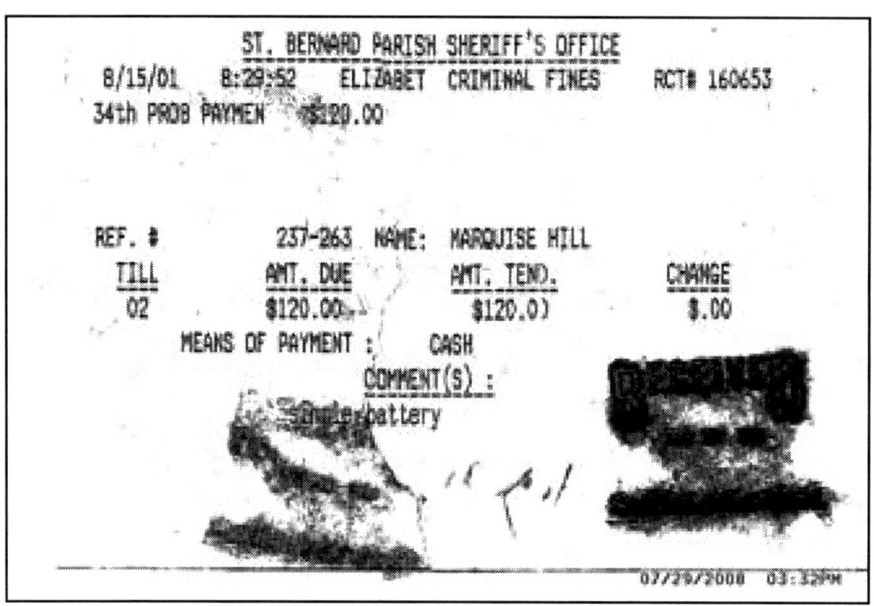
ST. BERNARD PARISH SHERIFF'S OFFICE

8/15/01 8:29:52 ELIZABET CRIMINAL FINES RCT# 160653

34th PROB PAYMEN $120.00

REF. # 237-263 NAME: MARQUISE HILL

TILL	AMT. DUE	AMT. TEND.	CHANGE
02	$120.00	$120.0)	$.00

MEANS OF PAYMENT : CASH

COMMENT(S) :

Simple battery

Court document salvaged from Katrina. My son was ordered to do community service on the highway (picking up trash). I refused to allow this to happen. I requested that his community service be done at the New Orleans Police Department while I was working there as a counselor. After that experience, Marquise would volunteer his time with troubled youth whenever he was home. I still have a photo of my son sitting with a student at the police station after one of his speaking sessions.

Often Marquise held "talk sessions" with troubled youth and first time offenders at the Juvenile Division, New Orleans Police Department. When the word was out that he was coming many parents made special arrangements with Headquarters to let their child listen in. He would sign autographs and take pictures after the question and answer period.

X

FINDING COMFORT IN A LESSON LEARNED

During the time I was going through the legal battle involving Marquise, I experienced an episode that had me almost afraid to walk through the door and out of my house. I started taking a peek outside my door to see if there was anybody coming before exiting.

Essentially, this is what happened.

One evening, I attended a friend's birthday party. I did not stay long, and I didn't drink any alcohol. At this time, crime was a huge issue in our city. When I got ready to leave, I noticed my car and another car behind it that looked just like mine—same color, same everything. My car was a wine/burgundy-color 1995 Dodge Spirit four-door. My friend had walked me out to say goodbye.

As I was talking to her and walking to my car at the same time, I was so distracted by what we were discussing that I did not notice which one I was going to because they both looked identical. I placed my key in the door, opened it, started the car, and got on the interstate.

At the back of my mind, a feeling started that something wasn't right. I started to notice that some things in the interior of the car looked different, such as, for example, a caddy lying on the floor. That was when a red light went off in my head, and I thought, *This is not my car!*

The first thing that came to my mind after that was that someone may already have reported a theft. I hurriedly turned around and returned to my friend's place to park the car into its previous parking space. When I arrived, I looked around to see if anyone had noticed anything strange going on and exited the car. I locked the car and took down the license plate.

I was hysterical over this incident, and for a long time I was hard on myself for making such a grave mistake. I may have blamed it on my state of mind at the time, but I did not want to hide behind any excuses.

Then, when the fog in my head cleared and my guilt trip was over, I started thinking seriously. What should never have happened is that my key should not have fit into another car anyway. So in a sense, it wasn't my fault but the car manufacturer's fault. So I called the main office to file a complaint, but they never gave me any satisfaction. I was told that as nothing serious had actually transpired, then there was nothing they could do.

After doing a little investigation of my own, I found that the identical set of keys should not have been placed in the same city. This is what was explained to me. The reason I had written the license plate number down was because I was going to find the person who owned that car to let them know that my keys fit their car, and I would also have assumed that their keys fit mine. The fact is that I do not want anyone to have the keys to my car.

The following week, however, my mother cleaned out the car and threw away the paper on which I had written the license plate number. I told my son about it, and he remembered part of that number—he had written it on a piece of paper too after I had told him what had happened. By the way, this also happened to be around the time when he was learning how to drive.

By the grace of God, I was traveling up the interstate one day, and I noticed a car that had a similar license number that seemed close to what my son said it was; so I followed the lady discretely to where she was going, which was a K&B on Read Road. I parked quite close to her, but she didn't notice that I was following until I told her who I was and why I wanted to speak to her. I let her know that I just wanted to try one thing, if she would be so kind as to lock her doors.

Thankfully, she cooperated. She locked the doors and I proceeded to open the door with my key. I even managed to start her car up with my key. Then I asked her to do the same with my car, but that didn't work. She also reported it to the car manufacturer, and they did nothing about it. I told her what had happen, and she confirmed that her car had been parked in that area at the time.

A lot of things could have happened to me because of a simple mistake. At that time, I was living in the murder capital of world, and someone could have mistaken my actions for stealing. If I had been dealing with the wrong individual, I could have been arrested for car theft. My car was left on the scene, registered under my address, of course; so my story may have been considered plausible.

But one never knows—I, of all people, was fully aware how the justice system could go awry at times. With all of the things going on in my life at the time, I certainly did not need something like this to happen to me. Luckily, that was the end of the episode, and nothing happened. With respect to the incident that happened to my son, however, he had not been so lucky. And he had not even made a mistake! Justifiable self-defense is not a mistake by any stretch of the imagination.

In Marquise's case, he was dealing with the dark side of humanity. Marquise realized from what happened that some people will simply live with hatred in their hearts and are not willing to change their outlook of the world. Therefore, it is not simply a case of racism; it is also a question of good and evil, of right and wrong. Marquise did not accept the minority idea; he would always insist that all humans are equal and that he had something to contribute to the world just like everybody else. He was color-blind and was proud to have friends of all ethnicities because that was the way I raised him. He felt that every man should have a backbone and be able to speak up for himself. The biggest issue my son had with people was when they crossed him and broke their word. In his mind, a man's word was his biggest treasure. If that treasure was depleted, so would be man's pride.

Sometimes, Marquise's wisdom would surprise even me. From a young age, he was a thinker, forever trying to figure out the mysteries of life. He would tell me things like: "Ma, you can't sprinkle water on my head and tell me it's raining"; "I don't dance unless I hear music"; "I always keep my grass cut low so I can see the snakes"; "Ma, I am of a different breed." He liked to talk so it made sense, so it would mean something. Life was not a game to him. It was a challenge to be overcome. On the football field, he fought his battles with sincerity and conviction, the same way he did in life.

With his teammates, he also liked to break tension with humor. The *Boston Herald* reported a comment he had made in an article printed after his death. Marquise's remark had made his teammates burst into laughter for days and days. This is what the article said, "During a rookie hazing skit with the Pats in 2004, he adlibbed that one of the strength coaches had such bad breath, 'I want to spread toothpaste on my fist and punch him in the mouth.'"

But even this desire to see laughter was a form of wisdom because he did it with a purpose. He thought that with a smile and a good laugh, anything could be achieved, and he lived by his word. After his passing, many of his teammates talked about this trait in him; it was one of those things that made a huge mark on their lives—apart from his determination, kindness, and compassion for others.

We had many conversations about life and the philosophy of living. My goal was to impart all the knowledge I had, but I also learned much from him. Whenever we discussed something and he lacked understanding of the question, he would say, "Please explain it to me like I am three years old"; and he would laugh that incredible, wholehearted laugh of his. Through all of these challenges, he began to mature in a leadership role. He was convinced that things always happened for a reason.

Graduating De La Salle High defensive tackle will be no pushover as LSU Tiger

By Victor Turner
Sports Writer

Marquise Hill is 6-8, 305 pounds. He runs a 4.9 in the 40-yard dash. He bench presses 370 pounds and squats 545 pounds. He averaged 14 points and 14 rebounds on the basketball team. This year, he was one of the most heavily recruited players to ever come out of high school in the nation. He also is academically qualified to play college sports and has already committed to Nick Saban and the LSU Tigers after starting off with 50-60 different colleges looking to recruit him. Marquise Hill is the real deal and his statistics in class and on the field can prove it.. This is all for a guy who didn't play football until he reached middle school. His position in middle school was quarterback, but now, with his massive frame, he is terrorizing opponents' backfields. Hill's numbers senior year: 87 solo stops, 31 assisted tackles, 14 sacks and 30 tackles behind the line of scrimmage. Hill recovered five fumbles and knocked down another four passes. By the way, he also blocked two punts and one field goal. "At 6-8 and 305 pounds, Hill is the most talented player I've ever coached," said De La Salle head coach Darren Barbier. "As talented as he is, I've had no problem with his character, work ethic and leadership. He's really down to earth."

Hill will graduate in the top half of his senior class and leaves behind a high school football resume that includes: National lineman of the year by Tom Lemmings of ESPN, Columbus (Ohio) Touchdown Club Player of the year, member of the *Times-Picayune* Top 16 Blue Chip list and he was rated the 7th best prospect in the nation by the *Dallas Morning News*, listed in the *Baton Rouge Advocate* Super Dozen and *Shreveport Times* Top 20 for the state of Louisiana and he was named first team 5A all-state.

Yet, with all the hype, Hill considers education the focal point in his life once he attends LSU. At LSU, Hill wants to major in pharmacy because he considers science to be his strongest subject. "A degree is No.1," said Hill. "If I can get a national championship, that would be cool, but I wouldn't die if I didn't. Hill believes that LSU was too good to pass up, as they were able to distance themselves from other colleges vying for his services. "Every school has their good points and their bad points. It's just the one that outweighs the others," said Hill. "There are no perfect people in the world and there are no perfect schools, either."

Hill has high expectations this season under Saban's guidance and is determined to show others how important college is to him. Hill understands his abilities and his accomplishments and refuses to forget where he came from and the promising future he has ahead of him.

Marquise Hill was scheduled to sign autographs with the champions at the Hilton on Saturday, April 7, for the Leukemia Foundation.0

News Clipping from the Louisiana Weekly Newspaper.

He felt whole when he supported a good cause. As I never tire of stressing, I believe he was a born philanthropist. When he helped others, he didn't question the where or why or how—he just did it, putting all of himself into it. I don't think I had ever seen anything like that before, and just watching him interact with others in these scenarios gave me unbridled joy. His first autograph signing was with the Leukaemia Foundation, and at the time, he was just out of high school. He had fun with the children, and we donated some of his paraphernalia to the organization. I wrote to *Louisiana Weekly* to inform them of Marquise's accomplishments as an athlete at such a young age and his desire to help others. The *Louisiana Weekly* editor and staff were wonderful to deal with.

At that time, my son needed special encouragement from the community—especially because of the disappointments he had just experienced. The support came in droves, and I will be eternally grateful because it put a genuine smile on his face. Although public recognition was not his priority, he did like to know that others felt love and appreciation for him, especially when he was going through some bad times.

First autograph signing at the Convention Center for the Leukaemia Foundation

Attention came not only from the public but also from the news media. I clearly remember an incident during Marquise's senior year, which happened in December 2000. Marquise and I were on our way to the airport to fly to

Atlanta as Marquise was to be a guest on *Countdown to Signing Day* on Fox Sports Atlanta. Unbeknownst to us, there was construction going on in the interstate. We had left forty-five minutes early; but because of the construction mess, I missed the exit, after which we only had fifteen minutes to get to the airport.

Naturally, I felt upset and guilty because this was my son's dream come true, and I was going to be the one to crush it. He had actually given up, and he wanted me to turn around and go back home because we had already gone too far out of the way. I could see he was disappointed, but he tried not to show it. I told him not to worry and that I would get him to the airport on time. I wished I believed my own words, but I hated to do or say anything negative to him.

I was hoping and praying that we'd make it. I did not know how I would have explained me causing him to miss an important flight. Regretfully, I have to say that I broke the speed limit that day, and probably some other road rules; but I couldn't take any chances. I drove farther down to get close to the following exit and made a U-turn. We did make it, at the expense of my blood pressure, of course. But it was worth it, as I still have some cherished memories of that interview—a photo and tape recording that I hold very dear.

Countdown to Signing Day—Fox Sports TV. Marquise was flown to Atlanta to appear on the show.

He had in fact considerable coverage from the local newspapers over the years; but I must say that perhaps the best and most poignant came after his accident, his death, and his funeral. I have kept all this literature, but it is still very hard for me to look at it—the grief overwhelms me. Nonetheless, I appreciate the respect that so many people showed me and my son and the kindness of their words. I will hold these messages always close to my heart.

I always held hope alive in my life. It gave both me and Marquise the courage and strength to fight. Even when I was going through all of the legal battles with Marquise and his cousin, Dewayne, I somehow wound up in church one night with a burdened heart. I knew there had to be some answers, and I was in the right place to find some.

I remember that day Pastor Morton's sermon was about "knowing your AI—the little you against the giants" (from the Scriptures: Joshua/ Numbers). It felt at that moment like he was talking to me, only to me. Sometimes, he said, "It feels like you are fighting a losing battle because you are up against some pretty tough giants." He continued, "However, with you and God together along for the ride, you would be on the majority side. With God in your corner, you are the winner, and the battle has been won because God fights the battle for you."

While we were going through all of this, Marquise would tell me, "Ma, things like this happen to the people in the movies. They shouldn't happen to us. All my life, I've tried to stay away from trouble and then got arrested because of the color of my skin. I ignored all that because that's what you always taught us." I used to repeat the saying to him, "Sticks and stones may break my bones (but words will never hurt me)."

He also told me, "I was attacked because I walked off and did not entertain it, but I was the one who had to get in the police car with the handcuffs around my wrist just because I defended myself."

After all this was over, he determined not to subject to this kind of abuse any more. He would speak out from then on. Marquise's experiences gave him a certain boldness in life. He had a tendency to speak out when he felt it was unfair, and he thought that a person's word was his bond. If one can give one's word without backing it up with action, he believed that was an unacceptable trait that needed to be addressed.

It may have surprised many people to see this radical change in him. When he was drafted, in fact, it surfaced that Marquise may have been bipolar. However, it did not matter to him what others thought because some of those people, he believed, never played this game of life that our family had lived. His fans and family were what ultimately mattered to him most.

He would always reassure me in his gentlest tone, “Ma, you worry too much. Don’t worry about me. When my time is up and I have to go, you live on. I am not destined to live long anyway. Football players usually don’t live long.”

He would tell me these words, and I’d never realize how prophetic they were. When I remember what he said that day, I feel goose bumps on my skin. I will always cherish our time together.

Marquise's last high school game at DeLaSalle. This photo was taken during halftime. From left to right, my brother James (deceased), Big Mom (my Mother), Marquise and I. He presented a Rose to my mother and me at mid-field before taking the photo. It is a school tradition during the last game for all senior players to show this way their appreciation to their parents at the end of the football season.

XI

FROM THE RECRUITING PROCESS TO GRADUATION TO DEATH VALLEY DAYS

In the month of May of 2001, we were gearing up for high school graduation at DeLaSalle, which was another milestone in my son's life. It was important that he graduate and be academically qualified for college. He took the ACT test more than once, and he began taking it early so he could increase his score.

He was such a perfectionist! He was adamant that the media would not be able to say that Marquise Hill has received many scholarships but could not pass the test. He never wanted to be classified stereotypically according to the general belief that "dumb" black men from the ghetto can play ball but cannot read or write so much as their own name. He wanted to be the one to break that perception and, as a result, be a positive role model for others like him.

He could not understand why any young black man, with all the education available to the kids today, would refuse to take advantage of this blessing and strive to better himself. Such an attitude and outlook on life, he believed, has set our race back a hundred years or more. He wanted to be an example for others to follow, not an embarrassment that needs to be forgotten and swept under the carpet of time. He wanted his family and friends to be proud of him. For this reason, he never stopped working hard. In the end, he graduated in the top half of his class, and his ambition was to major in pharmacy.

While he worked hard academically, he pushed himself athletically. At six feet eight inches (he had grown some more since middle school), approximately three hundred pounds in weight, he would run 4.9 in the forty-yard dash, bench press 370 pounds, and squat 545 pounds. Since his middle-school days, where sports was concerned, he dedicated his life to football. His considerably growing frame led the move from a quarterback

Hotbeds: New Orleans and the Northshore

Crescent City Has "Marquise" Player In Hill; Depth Is Lacking

by Scott McKay

It's not what you'd call a great year in New Orleans, but at least there's a marquee player.

Make that a Marquise player, as in De La Salle defensive lineman **Marquise Hill.**

At 6-8 and 305, Hill is "the most talented player I've ever coached," said De La Salle head coach Darren Barbier. "He really is a special person. As talented as he is, I've had no problem with his character, work ethic and leadership. He's really down to earth."

Last season Hill had 87 solo tackles, 31 assists and 14 sacks, including more than 30 tackles behind the line. He recovered five fumbles and swatted down another four passes.

Those numbers weren't just a product of his size. Hill sports a 29.5-inch vertical leap and runs the 40 in 5.0.

Where's this guy going to college? Anywhere he wants.

"Everybody in America is recruiting him," Barbier said. "But the discussion (of where he's going to college) hasn't even come up."

Barbier, who has a lot of experience with the recruiting process as an assistant at Archbishop Shaw and at Tulane and also as a head coach at Hahnville and Nicholls State, said Hill will take the recruiting process slowly. He's expected to pare his list down to eight or ten schools by October. The early favorites include LSU, Michigan, Texas and Florida State.

If there's anything the big guy needs to work on, it's his technique. "He got by on athletic ability a lot last year," said Barbier. "He needs to be a better technician, because sometimes the shorter kids can get up inside the bigger ones."

De La Salle defensive tackle Marquise Hill is the top player in an otherwise so-so class of New Orleans-area recruits.

Hill's recruitment is a fine way for LSU assistant Pete Jenkins to break back into the New Orleans area. Jenkins, who recruited such Tiger stars as John Hazard, Ron Sancho, Darren Malborough and Tommy Clapp out of the Catholic League during his previous stint with the LSU staff, is working or bringing Hill to TigerTown. Barbier says he's a big asset to the Tigers.

"Pete's a good guy. I've known him a while," said the coach. "LSU's definitely in the thick of things."

Outside of Hill, it looks like most of the action in metro New Orleans is on the north shore of Lake Pontchartrain this year.

In Slidell, Salmen quarterback **Tristan Smith,** a two-time all-district selection, is one of the state's most electrifying players. With a 40 time clocked under 4.4, the 6-0, 175-pound Smith has the speed to play wide receiver or cornerback at the major-college level.

In Tangipahoa Parish, three prospects are generating lots of attention - Independence offensive lineman **Aaron Lips** (6-5, 265), Hammond wide receiver **D.J. Jackson** (6-0, 190) and Amite defensive back **Jarrell Carter** (5-10, 185).

An old-school line prospect, Lips has a terrific frame and excellent mobility, having been clocked under 5.0 in the 40 at one camp this summer. He's been a starter since his sophomore year, when he first caught the eyes of the recruiting community by outplaying Evangel All-American Cole Pittman in the Class 3A state title game. Since that time, Lips has progressed to an All-District selection as a junior in 1999 and appears to be one of the state's top three line prospects this year.

Jackson, who hauled in 11 touchdown passes among his 45 receptions for Hammond last year, is a player whose stock rose during the summer camp circuit. Florida State, Tennessee, LSU, Ole Miss and Tulane appeared to be among his top options in the early going. One stumbling block to his progress, however, could be academics.

Amite's Carter burst on the scene in the Class 3A state title game last year, when he helped lead the Warriors in a 41-7 rout over Karr. Carter, who transferred to Amite from Hammond prior to his junior year, capped off an All-District season with a strong performance in that championship contest – including one vicious hit which knocked out both a Karr receiver and a teammate who happened to be running near the play. He's a little on the short side for a modern-day defensive back, but Carter's stock is on the rise nonetheless.

The Northshore area also has several potential sleepers, among them the Ponchatoula duo of defensive back **Roderick Livers**

News clipping by Scott Mckay salvaged from Katrina. Marquise lost hundreds Of Newspaper Clippings in Katrina Storm.

LSU, other top schools want to claim Hill

By David Whitmore

NEW ORLEANS — Florida State, Ohio State, LSU, Michigan, Notre Dame, just to name a few.

News clipping by David Whitmore, Salvage from Katrina.

position to a backfielder. As a senior, he recorded ninety-two tackles, eight sacks, and seven quarterback hurries. He also recovered five fumbles, knocked down four passes, and blocked two punts and one field goal. He loved the game. He lived it. That was just how committed he was.

Marquise was loved by all, including his coach. In an interview for a newspaper, made just after his graduation from DeLaSalle, Coach Darren Barbier caught Marquise's very essence when he said, "At six feet eight and 305 pounds, Hill is the most talented player I've ever coached. He really is a special person. As talented as he is, I've had no problem with his character, work ethic, and leadership. He's really down-to-earth."

- selected as National Lineman of the Year by Tom Lemmings of ESPN (and by several national publications)
- named the Columbus (Ohio) Touchdown Club Player of the Year
- named First Team All-American by numerous publications, including ESPN, *USA Today*, *Sporting News*, Rivals.com, SuperPrep, and Fox Sports
- became a member of the *Times-Picayune* Top 16 Blue Chip list
- received a rating as the seventh best prospect in the nation by SuperPrep
- rated as one of the Top 100 High School Players in the *Dallas Morning News*
- listed in the *Baton Rouge Advocate* Super Dozen
- listed in the *Shreveport Times* Top 20 for the State of Louisiana named first-team 5A All-state

These achievements were recognized and their stories published in several publications throughout the nation; I felt nothing but pride as a parent, not so much in the achievements themselves, but in Marquise's determination and willingness to take on responsibility and see things through. He brought me nothing but joy.

Again, I saw him give back to the community with a full heart, a young boy of barely eighteen who already knew what life was all about. Prior to graduation, in April of that same year, he was already signing autographs for the Leukemia Foundation. He would not pass up an opportunity to do something for sick or underprivileged children. I felt the luckiest mother in the world.

Graduation was a blast—it was one of those days one never forgets. A milestone, of course, in any mother's life. The family came over, and we were really happy that Marquise had reached this part of his life and overcame some significant hurdles on the way. Again, he still held the crown as the tallest young man in the class. His height was one attribute that everyone was aware of and was practically forced to notice.

Marquise signing *LSU* scholarship at school in the Library.
Standing—Mrs. Gelpi Marquise's grandmother, coach Barbier.
Seated—Marquise and I.

Press conference when signing scholarship.

From left to right Marquise's Big Mom, me, Marquise and
Ed Daniels, Marquise's favorite newsman.

Interview at DeLaSalle, after signing LSU scholarship papers.

DeLaSalle High School
Commencement
May 20, 2001.

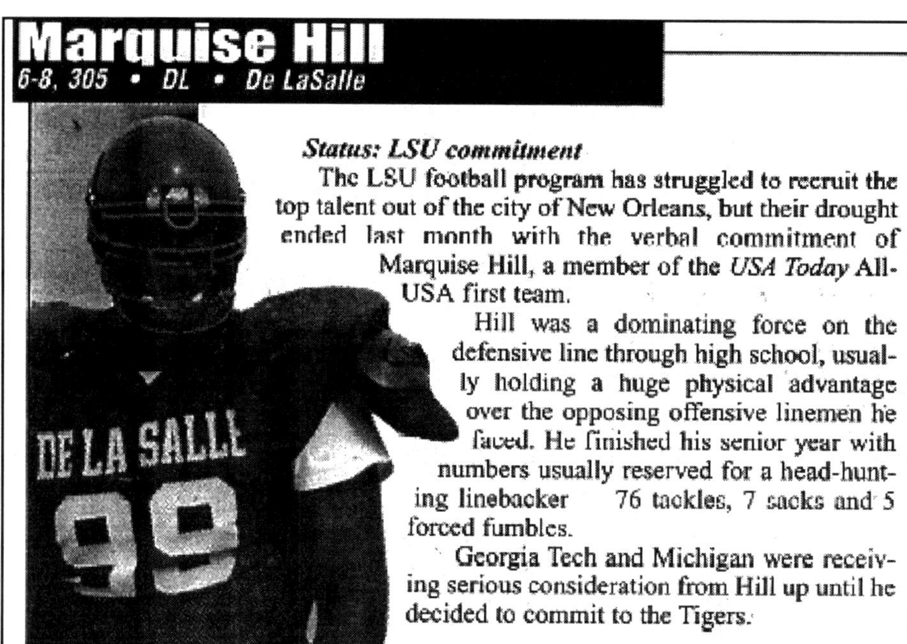

Marquise Hill

6-8, 305 • DL • De LaSalle

Status: LSU commitment

The LSU football program has struggled to recruit the top talent out of the city of New Orleans, but their drought ended last month with the verbal commitment of Marquise Hill, a member of the *USA Today* All-USA first team.

Hill was a dominating force on the defensive line through high school, usually holding a huge physical advantage over the opposing offensive linemen he faced. He finished his senior year with numbers usually reserved for a head-hunting linebacker 76 tackles, 7 sacks and 5 forced fumbles.

Georgia Tech and Michigan were receiving serious consideration from Hill up until he decided to commit to the Tigers.

News clipping salvaged from Katrina

Marquise's first big trophy. He flew out to Ohio to accept this award, It was the most prestigious award he was ever given, National Defensive player of the year presented by the Columbus Touchdown Club, and he was very proud of it. It was damaged during hurricane Katrina.

A detective showed up at my door after it became known that Marquise might be drafted into the NFL. At this time, my son made a settlement in the civil suit I discussed in the previous chapter. He did this because we were not legally represented, and he wanted to put this behind him. Of course, I did not cooperate with the settlement, but that was his decision nonetheless.

Once that was over and done with, better times were around the corner. Marquise was selected to attend Louisiana State University and thus made the transition to college football under the expert guidance of Coach Nick Saban, who took a liking to Marquise from the very start. Despite having played both offence and defense in the past, he was eventually recruited for the defensive line.

Marquise thoroughly enjoyed the recruiting process, which led up to his enrollment. The entire event was a roller coaster to him, but at the same time, he made his selection carefully. He weighed the pros and cons, and he finally decided that no other place would do for him but Louisiana.

Before his acceptance at LSU, however, he had been considering Michigan State University. In fact, he had over hundred scholarship offers and counting! Colleges called him, sent him letters (all of which I have kept in my box of treasured memories), and planned Marquise's visits. Coaches were vying for him like dogs would vie for a bone.

His coach, Darren Barbier, was lauding him as "one of the best in the country" with "a great work ethic" and "a real leader." He claimed there was nothing he would change about Marquise. My son was praised and cosseted throughout the length and breadth of the United States! He had always been surrounded by love in his life, but this kind of attention was an entirely different animal. He was determined to have as much fun as possible with it, but at the same time, he took it well in stride.

We traveled to Michigan for a visit, and I remember Marquise having problems hearing because it was his first time flying long-distance. Michigan had been one of his top choices, but the distance and the cold weather did make a difference in his final decision. He really wanted me to attend his games, and the necessity of flying back and forth would have been a major nuisance. In truth, I think he balked at the idea of being too far from home, family, and the Louisiana climes.

Notwithstanding his reservations, during his junior year at DeLaSalle, there were other schools he was thinking about. Apart from LSU and MSU, he had been leaning toward attending Florida State and Ohio State as well—above all else, he knew he wanted to attend a big school. He would always say that "Ohio got it going on."

At the same time, however, while he was going back and forth trying to decide on the different schools, LSU was always in the back of his mind, calling to him. Perhaps it was a call he was fated to answer, but certainly, it was a decision he never regretted.

In the meantime, prior to reaching his final decision, he kept visiting different campuses. Our visit to Michigan was made during his senior year. At the time, Nick Saban was in his second year there as a coach. This was before he joined the Alabama Crimson Tide. They immediately established a positive relationship based on mutual respect. I think this is one of those things that tipped the scales in LSU's favor in Marquise's mind. After our return from an enlightening trip, we went on to browse the LSU campus.

Marquise visited the LSU camp as well as the Nike Camp in Austin, Texas. Around the same time, in his senior year, my son also began a mentor-student relationship with Coach Kelly who was stationed at LSU. Later, the coach transferred to Georgia Tech, and my son decided to visit the school; so my mother and I accompanied him on that trip. Marquise liked both the Georgia Tech program and the structure of the curriculum. He would tell all future athletes to attend as many camps as possible because they would get a chance to see what they were competing against.

While traveling back to Louisiana from Atlanta, we passed through Birmingham and visited my brother, Marcus, who took us to the Alabama campus on an official visit. This was where my brother, an All-American LB, had played under Coach Bear Bryant.

It was during the dead season of recruiting that my son finally decided to select LSU, which recruitment was pushed forward by LSU defensive line coach Pete Jenkins. Marquise's decision caused the earth to shake from New Orleans to Baton Rouge. Many thought he would choose Michigan State, but truly, LSU was close to his heart. His freshman year brought out all the anxiety and stress from the twelfth-grade incident. He practiced hard and trained hard and played hard—repeating his unrelenting routine all over again.

Marquise's freshman year and his stint at LSU as defensive end was an exciting time for him. He gained a reputation as a powerful pass rusher, and his prospects as a defensive lineman were fantastic. His team won every game except one—a loss to Florida State—and he enjoyed every moment of this success. Another sophomore, Marcus Spears, was his roommate—theirs was an easy friendship. People called them Thunder and Lightning. Marquise was the former due to his large size, and Marcus earned the latter moniker, being the smaller and slightly faster one. Between them, they had vision to take the LSU Tigers to the next level.

Marquise took the games very seriously. In one interview, he expressed his amazing enthusiasm for the game of football, "We've got something to prove. We're just gonna bring it—that's all there is to it." This statement pretty much sums his attitude throughout the whole season. The media called him "a brick wall" and "a perfect combination of size, quickness, strength, and balance."

The championship game was held in New Orleans in 2003. It was another great game, and we celebrated with my son and his teammates. By this time, Marquise had collected five Bowl rings: (1) the All-American High School ring, (2) the Sugar Bowl ring, (3) the Cotton Bowl ring, (4) the SEC Conference ring, and (5) the Championship ring. Each one was a milestone for him and he was so proud of all of them!

Before the championship game, many reporters wanted to know what his plans were after for the future. Marquise told me, "Ma, I am taking one day at a time. I will have to make a decision depending on the outcome of this game. I have the heart to play another year, but I am also tired of you and my grandmother struggling. I was not born with a silver spoon in my mouth, and my father did not spoil me because I did not have a father. I made it through by the prayers of the righteous."

Marquise felt that the best way to enjoy one's days in life was to participate in a good game at the Death Valley stadium. He enjoyed the atmosphere and the wonderful energy from the fans. He would always say, "You are in trouble when you come to Death Valley." These events would turn him into a raging fire fueled by the heat emanating from the cheering audience.

Waiting on the clock after a Tiger Attack.

Tiger Attack in Death Valley.

"Trophy Kill" on Heisman Trophy winner in the championship game. In New Orleans, #16 OK Quarterback.

Marquise communicating with coach Saban on the sidelines during the Death Valley game.

Tiger Attack in Death Valley

Signing autographs on fan day in Death Valley
before the start of the season.

Death Valley Game.

But life at Death Valley was not all roses either. When one of his closest friends and coaches passed away, it really affected Marquise. Coach Jeff Boss would always give him words of encouragement when they performed the morning workout together. I had never seen him so sad until after the coach passed away. He took it very badly, and with his coach gone, he mourned the loss of a father figure who had meant the world in his life.

He would always say, “Ma, Coach Boss was a good person. He liked to do what’s right, and I admired him for that. I will never forget him.”

Interview before the championship game
by Ed Daniels, Channel 26.

Tiger attack ready stance position.

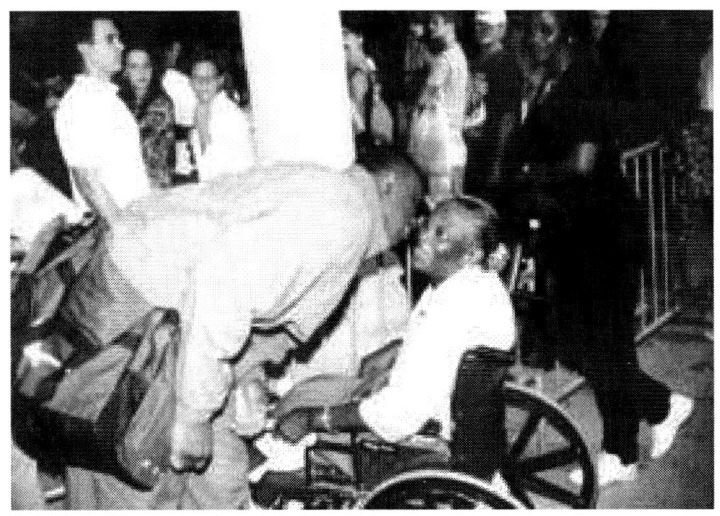

Kissing his Big Mom after the Death Valley Game. She had just been released a few days earlier after having knee replacement surgery but only missed one of his games.

Signing autographs after the Death Valley Game.

First Sugar Bowl debut as a freshman in New Orleans and LSU won. Marquise holding his cousins.

Marquise speaking at his old Alma Mater during the sports banquet.

A painting that I did of my son's first college Sack (Medium: Oil)
Marquise was very excited about the painting.
My son response "An artist for a Mom that's "TIGHT"
(Meaning Perfect in his Eyesight) "Thanks Ma"

Marquise was presented with a photo shoot of his famous plays while at LSU as a token of appreciation for speaking at the Banquet.

Marquise and Dewayne before they went their separate ways when they were young.

This picture was taken after Marquise and Dewayne reunited after Dewayne's release from prison following what we always believed to be a wrongful conviction in Alabama. Marquise was then a sophomore at LSU.

The first time Marquise stepped foot on the University of Alabama Stadium for the graduation ceremony for his uncle Marcus who played under Coach Bear Bryant

The last time Marquise stepped foot on University of Alabama soil as a player. This particular game was one of his best.

The Famous Tiger walk just before Death Valley Game.

Signing autographs after the Death Valley Game.

Fans Day before the season in Death Valley.

XII

DRAFT DAY IS A NEW DAY: THE BIRTH OF THE MILLION-DOLLAR MAN

Marquise cut a swath in the hearts of the fans and teammates. Before he had selected LSU as his alma mater, he ranked among the nation's Top 25 Football Prospects. Some scouts ranked him as the number 2 defensive lineman in the country. In our New Orleans neighborhood, he was the talk of the town.

However, what was important was that Marquise got what he desired at LSU: a great education and the opportunity to play football. That was his pragmatic, sensible side, which I'm sure he got from me and his grandmother. Or perhaps it had been those years that I had spent drilling into his head that he could do all he wanted as long as he got himself a decent education.

Despite the huge physical advantage he enjoyed, he played football like he played life—in a down-to-earth way. He was as hard a worker as they come because he knew that life didn't give handouts. He had to earn his kudos and earn them wisely. On a bio page posted on FOXStudentSports.com, he stresses the fact when he plays, "I don't listen to [the hype] because it distracts me. I just play my game. If you get caught up in the hype, you have a bad season . . . Trouble finds you when you're a football player."

When he said that, he sounded so much like me. If anyone knew about trouble and how it can find its way to one's doorstep when one least expects it, it was Marquise. Whatever he did, he never underestimated it. His absolute priority was to get a degree. At the same time, he had his dreams and goals, and he wouldn't let those go. He felt he didn't have to choose, that he could have it all if he applied himself enough.

After LSU, I knew that he would start looking toward his next greatest ambition—the chance to play in the NFL. He was thinking about it every day, his goal—the first thing he thought about when he woke up and the last thing he pondered when he went to sleep at night. He wanted to get there, not just for himself but also for our family.

Marquise's first visit to the White House when the President invited the Championship Team. His second visit was when his team won the Superbowl in Jacksonville the next year.

Accomplishments of

Mr. Marquise Hill

- Received over 100 Scholarship Offers Coming Out of High School
- Top Defensive Linemen in the Country ...ESPN's Tom Lemmings
- Received Ohio Touchdown Defensive High School Player of the Year
- Appeared on "FOX Sports Count Down to Signing National Sport Show"
- Played In The First High School All American High School Game in Texas
- Appeared in Several National Magazine and Web Sites Since High School
- Played on All Top Defensive Line in High School and College
- 3 Time Letterman at Louisiana State University
- Played in Three Bowl Games While at Louisiana State University
- Played on the National Chmpioship Team 2004 "Sugar Bowl"
- Received Three Bowl Rings
- Received National Championship Ring
- Plans to Receive His Degree During the Off Season
- Plans to Represent the National Football League

You are cordially invited to attend
an NFL Draft Celebration
With the Family and Friends of

MARQUISE HILL

Saturday, April 24, 2004
11:00 am to 8:00 pm
at
The Mile High Club
2901 Tulane Avenue
New Orleans, Louisiana
(Please present Admit Card and Identification to enter)

The NFL Draft Celebration invitation.

Draft day celebration came, and Marquise decided to head toward Texas for the draft selection after the championship game. This was his junior year when he decided to place his name in the draft and try his luck. Many thought it was too early, but his mind was made up, and I remember that his decision brought about much controversy. For a time, the news media wanted to portray him as deceitful and that his confusion was all an act. But all this was untrue. It caused much confusion in him. However, he was most of all a young man with a clear goal, and he was also aware of our family situation. For him, we came first—our happiness, our livelihood.

Many friends and fans wanted him to come back and play one more year. However, my son's decision for leaving early was based on personal reasons. He wanted to be able to provide for me and his grandmother, to give us all the life of comfort we never had. I never forced him to make a decision he wouldn't be happy with, but his sense of responsibility was too high; and when his mind was set, trying to change his mind was like trying to move a mountain or herding cats. He was as resolute as they come.

He was caught between a rock and a hard place. Shortly after all of this commotion, he began intense physical training to prepare himself for the draft. He sprained his ankle one time, and that cost him some precious seconds in one of his running tests. He was very upset about it, but he was not one to let these challenges in life stop him. He kept moving forward, pushing himself to the limit. In the end, he knew he would succeed.

The draft party was held at the Mile High Club on Tulane. Family and friends were all looking forward to this day; it was a dream day for everyone. I had invitations for the celebration made, as well as T-shirts with a picture of his famous quarterback sack imprinted on them for people to wear during the championship game. We had a large crowd; but as the hours passed, it died down, as did the revelry and good cheer. It was a long drawn-out day. Everybody was tired, and we thought the time would never come.

We all waited patiently to hear the news from Texas. We waited from 11:00 a.m. until 6:30 p.m.—and what we were waiting for finally arrived. Marquise was the final pick in the second round of the 2004 NFL Draft on April 24, 2004; over sixty young men had been picked by then. The news filled us all with a fresh wave of energy. When we spoke to him later, he was ecstatic and kept walking around as if lifted on a cloud. That was a day I will never forget. Such elation, such relief—my son had become a Patriot! He was officially signed on the twenty-third of June 2004.

After getting picked, Marquise boarded a jet from Texas to New Orleans to join us for the celebration. He couldn't wait to get there. We had an old-fashioned, honest-to-goodness New Orleans celebration, and his eyes sparkled with a new kind of pride. He had overcome all kinds of odds to get to this coveted place—"keeping his nose clean," as he'd say—and he was feeling an overwhelming sense of victory. Oh, he knew there would be more challenges to come; but after achieving such a break, he felt he could handle anything in the world.

After the party, everyone came over to my home, and we enjoyed the celebration until about four that morning. Everyone called him the MDM (Million-Dollar Man), and he laughed every time he heard that moniker. But I knew better—that nickname was no joke. It was Marquise's destiny; and the way he charged at life to reach his goals, never slowing down, he had nowhere to go but up—toward a phenomenal career in the NFL. A mother's certainty, you may think. Perhaps, but knowing his character and the way he put his heart and soul into everything he did, I could never doubt that success would be his for the taking.

Since the ninth grade, he had never broken his schedule. That was just how disciplined he was. How could he not succeed? He was happy to no end that now he would be able to support his family. Before getting to this place, he would talk about our struggles and tell me, "Ma, when you hurt, I hurt too."

At the end of the evening, I remember him coming to me and hugging me and whispering in my ear, "Ma, I finally made it. I told you I would. You can't keep a good man down."

XIII

THE ROAD TO THE SUPER BOWL

A few days after the draft ceremony, he began preparing for rookie camp. He never missed a beat. He kept working hard and training at all hours. When the season was over, his training continued. It always amazed me, the kind of discipline and self-control he had. He felt it was important to stay in shape at all times. He used to like to joke around and say that the NFL means "Not For Long." He knew his success depended on how conditioned and prepared he was for all those grueling games. He would take nothing for granted, least of all his livelihood.

In football, you have to take advantage of every moment and never let your guard down. You don't have time to waste. Some players play for the long term, and some players are forced to opt out early in their careers. One must stay focused and never lose sight of the main goal, which boils down to one simple fact: to bring the team to victory.

His first year with the Patriots was a challenging one. He always worked hard. He said it was a culture shock, and the transition from New Orleans to Boston was one that required him to adapt to largely different conditions. My son had never lived anywhere else other than in New Orleans. He was not used to the cold weather, which was an adjustment he had to make. The food was also different. He had never had clam chowder. Gumbo, shrimp po boy, jambalaya, stuffed crabs, crab fish bits, and red beans and rice with fried chicken were what he was used to eating.

As a result, he loved cooking Cajun meals for his friends in Boston. They would always tell me that Marquise was a good chef and could find his way around the kitchen. But I knew that his Big Mom was really the chef in our family, and he would always check with her, asking for her recipes and step-by-step instructions to making delicious meals. He couldn't help being a perfectionist in everything he did. He gave all of himself, no matter what he was doing.

As time passed, he adjusted well to his new home. He played one game that year, in 2004. During that game, he made a big play, unfortunately injuring one of the opponent's players. But his spirit soared, and he was inspired to keep improving himself. He kept his rigorous schedule both on and off-season. Off the field, he kept everyone entertained with his humor and laughter. It was contagious. *He* was contagious.

Meanwhile, he worked hard; the team made it to the play-offs and went to the Super Bowl. During this time, I felt compelled to return to my roots and give my life over to God. The Almighty One had given us hope—with him, we cannot be disappointed; and without him, we have nothing. In God, we have a formidable ally to fight our battles with. My life, therefore, also changed during Marquise's first year in the NFL.

We traveled to Boston with family and friends, to attend the event. We really enjoyed the festivities. It was like being in seventh heaven. My oldest brother, James, who is now deceased, also traveled with us. My son was very close to him. The Super Bowl ceremony was held on February 6, 2005, and it was a day I'll never forget. When we arrived, the limo picked us up from Marquise's condo for an evening of fun to celebrate the endowment of the Super Bowl ring.

Marquise and I waiting on the limo to take us to the Super Bowl Ceremony in Boston, 2005.

By this time, in fact, my son had purchased a three-story condo in Boston. After the Super Bowl and before Katrina, he also purchased a home for me in New Orleans, across from the Berg Canal. It was a two-story minimansion with spiral staircase. Before owning it, Marquise had dreamed it for many years. As per his dream, the house also featured a full bar and a couple of large-screen plasma TVs.

That day, the energy of the celebration was incredible; it was a time like no other. Marquise really cherished his Super Bowl ring (well, he loved all his rings which represented his accomplishments. The Super Bowl ring was only the last in a string of successes) and appreciated everything that he had achieved. Above all else, the ring signified the attainment of his ultimate goal, which was to make it to the Super Bowl. Sometimes I remember what Marquise used to say after this day, something about how the Super Bowl ring was "the only bling he ever cared about." I remember him also repeating this sentence in several interviews, and it rang so true. Marquise wasn't big on the material things, although he did have dreams and aspirations. Nonetheless, his favorite possessions were those which had some kind of meaning to him. A symbol of his team winning the Super Bowl certainly qualified as such.

As always, the energy at the game flowed through Marquise in much the same way a car is revved up by a powerful engine. Marquise was the car, and his fans were the engine. He was completely motivated by these people who believed in him so much, especially the elderly and the children. Their enthusiastic response to his presence and his plays kept him on a constant high, a place from which he never wanted to come down.

If he could make any person, particularly a child, feel special—that would make his day. I remember the times, when Marquise was a boy, when I could not afford to let him join any football summer camps. However, when I worked in the projects, Marquise had the opportunity to interact with some professional football players from the Saints team. They visited the preschool where I was employed as a center supervisor, and I took Marquise to meet them. Also, the Super Bowl was held in New Orleans one time, and that time we were able to partake in the festivities. At the time, he was about twelve or thirteen years old. It was the experience of a lifetime for him; and now that he was on the other side of the fence, from the inside looking out, it made the whole experience even more special.

Around this time, Marquise started heavily insisting on moving us into a bigger house. So he and I went searching for the right property. Just between the Super Bowl and Katrina, in 2005, he purchased a beautiful large house for me.

Marquise displaying his pride and joy—his BLING BLING!
A total of six rings, including the Super Bowl ring.
My Son accomplished in 23 years.

Marquise posing with Boston fans.

His favorite hobby—restoring old cars. Before and after pictures.

Then the hurricane came, and Marquise lost a lot of money on the house. The insurance was dropped, and we did not find out until afterward because Marquise thought he had everything straightened out. He had paid the insurance up front before the closing. I had put my signature at the closing, and it would not have been possible to do so without having insurance in place. We were told at the closing that the bank was responsible for the check, which was somehow "misplaced."

We felt that we had been cheated, and Marquise found it hard to accept. He was tolerant of many things, barring racism, prejudice, and greed. In this case, the problem was the latter. One day, we were discussing the problem; and he said one of his famous phrases, "Ma, that's the reason I keep my grass cut low . . . so I can see the snakes." Despite his better intentions, he hadn't seen the snakes coming this time.

So he drowned his frustrations in something else. During this time, Marquise finally had the required funds to indulge in a dream hobby of his—to purchase and refurbish old cars. He was an old spirit who loved Ray Charles, Otis Redding (his favorite ringtone happened to be "(Sittin' On) The Dock of the Bay"), and old gangster movies and documentaries. The Purple People Eaters of the 1970s Minnesota Vikings were also his favorite defense team. The *Boston Herald* printed this about my son after his passing—a concise, clear picture of who Marquise was. It was a natural progression that he would also come to love and be fascinated by old cars.

He became an enthusiastic collector. He would buy them and fix them up to his taste. He would have the paint job redone, as well as the interior (from top to bottom), the sound system, and anything else he felt needed be fixed on the exterior of the vehicle. It was his pleasure to take the cars out for Sunday drives and set them free on the highway or cruise around the city. He treated those machines with velvet gloves. He used to call each of them his Sunday Car.

He would purchase them and later resell them once he finished working the refurbishment process. Following the sale of one car, he would then proceed to buy another and give it the same amount of tender loving care, use it for a while, and then resell it. As the *Boston Herald* confirmed, one of his most prized possessions was indeed a refurbished 1967 Lincoln Continental. He had purchased this car for his grandmother; but today, because Marquise left no will, the car is in limbo, bunched up with the rest of his estate, which is still tied in litigation.

XIV

THE KATRINA EPISODE AND A TRAGEDY

In 2005, my son purchased a plane and game ticket for my brother, James, so he could attend a play-off game in Boston in November of 2005. This was two and a half months after Katrina. The hurricane had hit us hard that year. We lost most of our possessions. I remember Marquise had six large computer boxes stuffed full of memories; namely, his college scholarship offer letters, which we kept tucked away in our storage room. He was planning to make a collage out of these bits and pieces from his life, but he lost it all.

We lost most of our family pictures, bits and pieces of our lives that drifted away with the wind and the water along with our home. Thankfully, we managed to salvage a few tapes and other items that we could not have borne to lose. Basically, we had lost everything except a handful of things because my home had drowned in five feet of water. I had also lost my neighbor and other friends we had known for years.

However, more challenges were about to come our way. On the ninth of November, approximately six days before my brother's birthday on November 15, my mother and I received a call from his wife who told us to meet her at Summit Hospital immediately because my brother had been rushed to the emergency room.

James passed away soon thereafter, and Marquise was utterly devastated by his uncle's death; he even had his face tattooed on his arm. He said he punched two holes in his wall when he received the call. He could hardly believe his uncle James was gone. We had never lost anyone that close in our family before, so this was the first time that Marquise had had to deal with this kind of loss. Suffice it to say that barring Marquise's career, 2005 was a very difficult year for our family.

At the same time all this was happening, we had to deal with other issues in the aftermath of Hurricane Katrina, such as going back and forth with the insurance company, handling contractors who were charged with rebuilding the homes in New Orleans and their fraudulent actions, and other similar problems. People in New Orleans and the Gulf Coast area became like refugees from another world in the blink of an eye. That's the way a lot of people were feeling here back then. When my son came home to visit, we were living in a FEMA trailer; and when he saw the condition we were in, he became even more upset. He made the decision there and then that he would dedicate his energy to rebuilding people's homes. He could not give them the loved ones they had lost, but he could give them a roof over their head. He rolled up his sleeves and determined to fix my house so we could have a decent roof over our heads. We were living between Baton Rouge and New Orleans, but my job was still in New Orleans. I had no other choice but to travel through the week to go to work while my son worked on my home.

Justin and Jarrett Burney received the treat of their life in 2006. Their aunt asked my son if he would take some time to sign autographs for her nephews because they were his #1 fans. He gave them t-shirts from the Draft party and signed them. The remaining t-shirts were salvaged from Katrina. The boys' aunt stated that "Marquise made their day." We had been displaced to Baton Rouge because of Katrina when my son took time to fulfill this lady's request.

During the rebuilding process in New Orleans, Marquise was concerned about the citizens of the area who had nowhere to stay. He noticed how contractors were taking people's money and not doing the work they were supposed to be doing. It was like one disaster trying to patch another. Many of these contractors charged overblown prices, and contract fraud was the order of the day, not the exception. Marquise became much obsessed with these issues and took it upon himself to make a difference and bring in some order. Besides his proactive work in the community, if he found a contractor who was fair and decent, he would always refer the company to others who needed help with their homes.

Prior to Marquise's death in May of 2007, he was in the process of buying homes for the people of New Orleans because families wanted to return home but had nowhere to live. He always made himself available to offer his assistance to any parent or child in need. My son would tell me and promise me that if he ever made it to the big league, he would never change. He never lost touch with his roots and his family. He put his faith in God and respected the lessons he had learned. He said that many friends he grew up with would tell him he changed; but he would always respond to them, "I didn't change, my bank account changed. That's the only thing that changed in my life and within myself."

Prior to the havoc wreaked by Katrina, I worked with the juvenile division, and Marquise volunteered many times to attend and speak to the young people about making the right choices. We would usually invite him in to speak to first-time offenders; but because he was so popular, the word would spread in the neighborhood, and many parents would bring their children in anyway just to let them hear him talk about his career (See photos on page 85).

At these little seminars, he would speak out about the importance of staying in school and getting a good education. The youngsters' parents preapproved all the speaking sessions. He would take any and all opportunities he was given to tell the young people to stop making excuses and using them to justify bad behavior. Just because a boy does not have a father or his father is never at home doesn't mean he cannot live a good life and be a person everyone can be proud of. Marquise admitted to everyone that he had no father, but he still worked hard to become somebody, and others could do just like he did. He would tell them not to have a pity party. He'd say, "If life gives you lemons, don't waste time talking about how sour they taste, just go ahead and make some lemonade."

After the Katrina episode and eight months after the Patriots' Super Bowl win on August 31, 2005, something beautiful and entirely unplanned entered Marquise's life: his baby son. The boy's name happens to be a blending of Marquise's name and mine. He was the apple of Marquise's eye, a little bundle of joy he loved to call Mini Me, and my son loved him with all his being. He was scared of calling him simply Marquise because he was concerned it would put undue pressure on the little boy, and on himself, to live up to some impossibly high standard. He wanted his son to have all the love and happiness in the world. In his eyes, being happy was more important than success.

My old house before Katrina.

Front of old house After Katrina.

A backyard view behind my old House after Katrina

The home Marquise purchased for me.
The photo was taken after Katrina and before renovation

Front and Back view of the house after renovation
The house featured a lake in the back, a 12 foot pool and a Gazebo on the lake. My son had told me that this house would be temporary until after his next contract. God willing, he said, he'd build me one from the ground up. My friends and relatives called this house a "mini-mansion."

He said that having a son made him have a better outlook on life as a whole. I think he's always been a positive young man; but this little boy brought all the love, tender compassion, and responsibility into a much bigger focus. About a year before his death, my son and his girlfriend had gone separate ways. Because of several reasons, he told me that he felt the relationship was not "it" for him so he chose to pursue the life of a single person.

Despite everything, he would do the right thing. For six months, she had her own apartment, after which she chose to move to Texas with her parents to finish school. Marquise gave her a BMW to make her life easier. He did not want his son to lack anything he may need, and that also meant taking care of the mother and easing her path so his son would not want.

Marquise would tell me, "Ma, I am not going to abandon my son like my father did with me. My son will know me because I will make sure that I will always be in his life as long as I am living. Since he has come into my life, I can't see how a father can walk away and not take care of his responsibility. Men seem to be only sperm donors and not real fathers."

He would tell me that he had no intention of marrying anyone before the end of his football career because he wanted to stay focused, but that would not prevent him from caring for his son the way a real father should. And he kept his promise. As always, he believed in values and being real and letting one's word be one's bond.

Marquise proved to me again that he was wise beyond his years. He wanted to prepare for his son's future, so he did not waste his money. He was quite conservative with his spending. He had been told once, "Always watch your pennies, and your dollars will take care of themselves." He lived by this saying. We had talked about "preparing for the future" before his death, yet the tragedy came with no warning. Today, Marquise's estate is a matter of contention. I fervently wished it wouldn't come to this, but where the lure of money is concerned, greed becomes a blinding influence on many. In the past long months, I have witnessed this ugliness firsthand.

Years ago, I heard someone say something about why erasers are made. It seems that there's a saying, which goes something like: if you have a conscience, then that should be your eraser in life. If you make mistakes, your conscience will make you correct them. However, for this to happen, one's heart must be in the right place. For some, I regret to say, this will never be an option.

That said, I'm happy for all the precious moments I was allowed to have with my son. Sometimes the memories wash over me like languid waves slowly rolling toward the shore on a warm summer afternoon.

At this moment, I'm remembering the last birthday I celebrated with him. He took me on a long limo ride between Baton Rouge and New Orleans. It was a lovely afternoon in 2006. The area was still recovering from the effects of the hurricane—still, that was one of the best days of my life. It was one of many great days with my son.

That limo ride was the last we'd ever have together.

XV

THE JET SKI ACCIDENT

Marquise's career was unfolding. His lifelong dream had been achieved—to be a part of the Patriot's Super Bowl XXXIX Championship team. It was a great thing to achieve for someone who hadn't been on the team long. In his first three seasons with the Patriots, he played thirteen games, which was welcome after an inactive rookie season. In 2005 and 2006, his role was that of a reserve defensive lineman, but it meant a lot to him that after the first year, he still had a chance to play a few games. He was looking forward to becoming an even better athlete and playing many more games in the immediate future.

But some things are not meant to be.

On May 23, 2007, at approximately 9:00 to 10:00 p.m., my son arrived at my house for a few days of relaxation. It was Memorial holiday weekend, and his arrival was on a Thursday. That same night he told us about a bad experience he had just had the night before he left Boston.

He told me and his grandmother, "Mom and Big Mom, I had a bad night with Uncle James just before I left. I looked at the tattoo of his face on my arm, and I just started crying. It seemed like I couldn't stop. I didn't understand it." He seemed very perturbed by the whole experience, but after a while, he left to go and check on the workers at the other house we were fixing post-Katrina and hoping to finish soon. He had also been buying and sorting construction materials, as well as working on another house, which he was fixing for some people who had lost their home in the disaster. He knew that would keep him busy for a while, and it seemed that he soon forgot about his dream. He never mentioned the incident anymore, and we did not want to bring it up again either.

That Friday, on the twenty-sixth of May, he worked on the other house all day, trying to get it finished before he returned to camp. In fact, I hardly saw him that day as work was a priority on his mind. Late that evening, he told me about an old classmate he had met that day. She was rebuilding her house, and she was having problems with uncooperative contractors. He told her he was going to see what he could do to assist her.

The following day, on Saturday morning around eleven, Marquise said to me, "Ma, I want you to see this movie about an athlete who would have been all-time if he would have made it to the basketball league. He was a baller." The movie really affected him because the story hit close to home. The main character was caught up in the system, and that prevented him from achieving the success he wanted.

Later that night, we talked for over two hours about a lot of things that had happened over the past twenty-four years; and we talked about our hope that the next year would be a good year, which would, God willing, not bring so many challenges. We talked about everything under the sun. Mostly, he wanted to talk about his son, a gift that had come into his life without warning, like a thunderbolt ripping the sky on a clear day. It was one of those things he knew he'd never regret, as his son brought much joy into his life.

The last few words he told me will always remain close to my heart and in the forefront of my mind, "Ma, man can't play God. Everyone must give an accounting of what they do, and that is the reason why I try to do the right thing. I want to treat people right." He felt that the next year would bring much happiness and good fortune to him, and many years of hard work and training would pay off. While other athletes took vacations, he would keep on working, honing his physical abilities, without claiming any respite or complaining about his choices.

He was always good on prediction, and I gave a lot of weight to his words. He had an uncanny sort of wisdom, sometimes too much to handle for one so young. He had grown up in a hard, unforgiving environment, but he had known much love from those closest to him; and because of this, he grew fast and strong. He sometimes got philosophical and wistful about it, yet when it got too much, he'd lighten the mood and cheerfully declare, "I believe we have a chance to go to the Super Bowl again this year."

That evening, after our heart-to-heart, he started getting ready to go out. I ironed a shirt for him, but after a while, he decided to change to another outfit. He wanted to look his best that night. He had been invited to attend a private gathering with another NFL athlete, and he told me he did not want to miss it, but he would be back early.

I saw him again on Sunday morning after he got up because I went to bed upon his departure the previous night and never heard him come in. That day, he was planning to meet his uncle Aaron, who was due to arrive in New Orleans from Houston in the early afternoon, and they were going to work at the house together. Marquise was due at camp the following Wednesday, so his goal was to finish the repairs before his departure. When my brother arrived at the location, Marquise was helping the contractors lay down the tile in the kitchen. He gave money to the contractor so they could go out and get them some beer and fruit juice for him. They had a few toasts and laughed and talked all day. Marquise was in a good, cheerful mood.

Later he came and picked me up from the new house he purchased for me before Katrina and took me by the old house I had been living in before the hurricane struck. Just before Katrina, after he'd purchased the new home for me, he started renovating it. He took me there to observe the contractor's progress while the men were working, and to give him my opinion of how it looked. He loved the stuccoed effect, which is why he chose to renovate and finish the home a certain way., that was the last time I saw him alive, the accident occurred on the 27th of May. That year(2007) would have been his fourth year in the NFL.

He went to the lake; that was the last time I saw him. This wasn't the first time Marquise had gone to the lake. Since childhood, it had been one of his favorite haunts when he wanted to get away from everything. At approximately eight thirty that same evening, I received the fateful phone call when an officer (Coast Guard) broke the news to me. I was told I needed to go to the Seabrook Bridge because my son—my hero, my everything—had just been involved in a jet ski accident. I arrived at the lake around nine thirty, but I could not stay out there too long because I was so heartbroken. It was the twenty-seventh of May when my son died, but his body was found a day later, on Memorial Day.

I later found out that he did not have a life jacket on, which is illegal in Louisiana, but I would have rather seen him get a ticket and a police officer slapping a pair of handcuffs around his wrist than face what had actually happened. I also found out that he died to save the life of another.

When his friend was thrown off the Yamaha WaveRunner by the unforgiving waves as they steered around toward the south shore of Lake Pontchartrain, he stepped into action. The jet ski had flipped over, and Ashley panicked because she wasn't as good a swimmer as Marquise.

Promptly, Marquise guided her to a piling in the water and told her how to hold on. However, the currents were so strong that day that he never made it to safety; and he drifted into the deep waters, sucked into the vortex created by fast, swirling currents. Perhaps no amount of skill as a swimmer could have saved him that day as he also hit his head as he fell, and the autopsy concluded he might have experienced the effects of a concussion before he died. It all happened very fast in the vicinity of the Seabrook Bridge, and it was very dark at the time at 9:00 p.m.

Subsequently, Marquise's friend, after her calls for help were heard, was rescued by some boaters who happened to be nearby. They had also seen Marquise trying to save himself for a few seconds just before he disappeared into the pitch-dark waters. Someone had even tried to toss a rope at him, but it was too late. The Coast Guard arrived about thirty minutes later, and rescue teams were dispatched. By then, however, Marquise was gone. The following day, they recovered his body. His head was bruised from the hit he had taken.

I am pleading to anyone who enjoys swimming or jet skiing, whether in a lake, pool, or a bucket of water—please wear a life jacket! I know of an incident when a baby actually drowned in a bucket of water, so I'm not trying to make a joke. Anything is possible; and life, being unpredictable the way it is, gives no quarter.

I cannot question God, but the day my son lost his life was the day the joy left my heart. I was in a daze for days, and in many respects, I still am. I sometimes wake up thinking I'm going to hear Marquise's voice booming from his old bedroom or the other end of the phone line.

The funeral was a difficult day to live for me. The only way I could go through it was if I put my mind in another place and time, yet the tears kept streaming down my face and the searing pain wouldn't quit. A dreadful melancholy settled inside me; and in many ways, it's still there, lodged deep in me, to this day. I've come to think it will never go away, but writing this book has been cathartic for me. It was the best thing I could have done to make my son's passing meaningful and share it with the rest of the world.

The church (Greater St. Stephen Full Gospel Baptist Church in the uptown neighborhood, of which both Marquise and I were members) was full to the brim with people from all over the country—the Louisiana State University team, Marquise's high school and college friends, relatives, and people from our hometown—who came to say their last goodbyes. Mr. and Mrs. Kraft, as well as the New England Patriots and the team administration flew in for the wake but had to return for practice. They did not stay for the funeral. Nonetheless, I saw many of my friends and coworkers, as well as Marquise's high school principal, Ms. Hall, who loved him like a son. I had never seen so many people in a funeral as long as I have lived.

Yet nothing could have filled the emptiness in my heart.

Bishop Paul Morton gave a very moving sermon. He told everyone that day that Marquise was now on heaven's team, and that team could never lose a game. He talked about my son and described him as a winner, especially in the game of life, family, friends, and spirit. The coverage of the circumstances of his death and the funeral was immense. Even today, if one looks up the Internet for information about my son, one can find countless articles, which talk about him, how he died, and the person that he was.

One of the most moving moments was when Bishop Morton spoke on behalf of Marquise, as if he was talking to us from heaven: "I've fought a good fight. I'm going to miss my team, and God knows I'm going to miss my family. I can see him out on the water saying, 'I'm ready!'"

His teammates were all in shock, but many of them said that what Marquise had done was very much in character. He was known by all as someone who would help others, and with his last action, we all found that he'd do it at the cost of his life. He died a hero, a man so many people looked up to.

Patriot defensive end, Jarvis Green, talked about how Marquise made everybody laugh; and he was sure my boy was smiling at us from heaven that day. People leaned on him because he knew how to break the tension and make everyone feel like a million bucks. He described Marquise as a person who "gave his all," the consummate hard worker and a role model for everyone. He thought of others more than he thought of himself—one need only look at the way he died. LSU teammates, Chad Lavalais and Corey Webster, also said their piece. These young men were scattered about the country now, all following their dream of a pro football career, but they had never forgotten Marquise's smile and dedication. At his funeral, their love and respect shone through. They saw his death as the reflection of a man who was honorable and giving.

Oh, I hate to admit this, but how I wish he had been selfish that day! As a mother, I'd have given anything if only he could have been returned to me alive and well! If he had given a little more thought to his life, he would still be with me today and I'd be writing this book with him, the way we had been planning to do for a while. But how can I hate him for doing what he did? For God to have given me my wish would have meant that Marquise couldn't have been true to himself. Saving the lady at the lake was his priority in that moment, that split second that determined his fate forever. I couldn't have expected him to accept someone else losing their life than his instead.

At the funeral, however, with all those people around me, it was hard to come to terms with reality. I watched Cincinnati Bengals center Ben Wilkerson, a close friend of Marquise and a pallbearer at the funeral. He was also a college roommate and LSU teammate. When he spoke, he spoke directly to me. He said, "Ms. Hill, you lost a son, but if you look to your right, you have so many more sons over there." I looked at Ben and all the other teammates; I looked at my son's polished casket, glistening and covered with red roses, then at the action photo depicting him during an LSU game; and I completely broke down.

And today, here I am, penning my son's testimony as if it were his own, yet still from the eyes of a grieving mother. I feel like a fraud because he should have been the one to do this—to be here, typing away, telling you about his life's adventures. Now I have taken his place because that is what he would have wished.

This is his legacy, one that will move on to his son. I hope that my grandson will know his father more through the pages in this book. I hope that when he grows up, he becomes a man his daddy would be proud of. Marquise's blood runs strong and true through this little boy's veins, bathing him with his spirit. And in this beautiful little boy, I know and feel in my heart my beloved Marquise lives on.

Images from Marquise's funeral.

I received words of comfort from Coach Sam Nader and LSU Coach Les Miles.

Marquise's former Teammate at LSU Ben Wilkerson.

Bishop Paul S. Morton singing one of Marquise's favorite songs, "*Your Tears.*"

Bishop Morton and Pastor "D" Deborah Morton.

XVI

NOT A FAIRY-TALE ENDING

NOTE TO THE READER: In this and other chapters herein, Darrell Jackson and Janice Meeks are fictitious names for real people. Their names have been changed to protect their privacy.

Marquise's passing has not only created pain but has also brought about rifts where there should be family unity. Unfortunately, Marquise died before writing his will. There are many more obstacles I do not look forward to facing at the time of this writing, and I hope that things will be resolved as Marquise would have willed. So far, I have had no assistance from the legal angle, being that I was cheated from a goodly sum from my own attorney—$7,500 to be precise, which, to me, is a lot of money.

When Marquise died, I needed to procure some legal representation, but I waited for a while before I did so. In fact, after putting my trust in the wrong people and being lied to many times over by those people, it took me a while to regroup. When I did hire a lawyer, he charged me a $7,500 retainer for fifty hours of work. He assured me that I had the right to seek to become administrator of Marquise's property. Unfortunately, a bigger fallacy was never told. Under the State of Louisiana, of course, everything goes to the son of the deceased. Which I would not have had a problem with, but seventeen days after his death, I was told by the attorney that my grandson's mother, Janice Meeks, had applied to the courts to become sole administrator of Marquise's assets. Basically, this was a lie because at the time she wasn't "applying" for this position; rather, she had *already* been appointed such. I found this out by reading an article in the *Boston Globe.* My attorney did not feel the importance of apprising me of this situation. I had to "read" it in a newspaper long after the fact, so until then I was totally in the dark. Today, I'm still working hard at getting a reimbursement and settling this frustrating issue against yet another attorney I couldn't trust.

One of the first things that happened to make me realize something was going on was my getting on a three-way call with myself, a man who my son trusted with his business affairs—Mr. Darrell Jackson—and the insurance company, which I will explain a little further down. As you will see, it was the event that finally made me "smell the funk."

I have always wondered, since then, what my son would have thought of all this. My mother and I would tell him about making a will, and he would tell us, "Darrell knows what I want." He thought that just because he had a conscience, then everyone else would have one. He was trusting, open and kind. Being older, we knew better that often one cannot depend on others this way, especially where money was concerned.

Unfortunately, we were proved right. As of the time of this writing, I'm somewhat at peace with the situation, albeit still experiencing moments of disillusionment and sadness, and I am placing it all in God's hands.

I was treated abominably by people who were close to my son at some point—people who, I believe, have nobody's interests at heart but their own. I may be wrong, and I certainly hope so, but all evidence points to the contrary. Before my discovery of the sole administrator being appointed for the estate right after the tragedy, I called Mr. Jackson and asked him for direction on how to proceed and get access to Marquise's records so I could have an idea of what was in the estate. I was so confused and still grieving, but I knew there were things that needed to be done. When I asked him that, he told me that I didn't have to do anything, but just sit and wait and "do nothing." This was actually the first instance which led me to feel misled.

Two days after the burial, however (around the time the application for sole administrator was filed), on June 4, he invited me on a three-way phone call with the benefits department at Marquise's insurance company. In another conversation, he also asked me why I had inquired about Marquise's house insurance. You got that right, he (who is *not* a beneficiary) was asking *me*—Marquise's mother—what business *I* had with the insurance company. During that call he asked me to fax him a power of attorney so he could settle things. I wondered whether I was crazy or had I really heard that request. But I had a witness so I know he actually *asked* for this document from me. During this time, he also asked if there was a will in place.

I was still grieving, and I would love to know why that call was made to me from the benefits office at that time, a mere two days after my son was put to rest by someone he trusted. This call was made despite the fact that I had already contacted the office to ask them not to release any information to anybody. I did not grasp the urgency of it because at that time, money was the last thing on my mind. How much can a grieving mother take?

At this point, I knew that man had landed on the moon and rockets could be launched into space—but pigs could not yet fly. So I politely told him that I would not give a power of attorney to anyone; if some signature was needed somewhere, any papers processed or information exchanged, I would personally take care of that. Would a person sign a contract without reading it or give a stranger access to a personal bank account? Incidentally, I had already specifically instructed the insurance company not to give out any information regarding my son to anyone other than to me. So my thoughts are, What was his intent when he called me that day? Why was he so insistent on me granting him a power of attorney?

The entire process was very confusing. I was not able to locate any funds in my son's business marketing account, which was very strange. I know that Marquise was not a wasteful person. He did spend money, but he also exercised wisdom and restraint. Most of his cars were paid for except two—on which he didn't owe much. After this strange occurrence, it was like a wall was erected and I had no access to any further information concerning Marquise's accounts. Sometimes, I feel that I was left out of the entire process because I was asking too many questions, making certain persons uncomfortable.

I also inquired about my son's football contract and house insurance which had been dropped during Katrina—and I was asked by Darrell Jackson *why* I wanted to know all this information. He told me there was no contract left and that I "wouldn't know what I would be looking at if I had a contract in my hand." Not quite the statement I was expecting.

During my conversations with Mr. Jackson, however, I was told by him that I should do absolutely nothing about this issue, that everything would be alright. I felt comfortable in my trust, although I did realize I had need for an attorney. Nonetheless, ten to fourteen days later, Janice became the administrator of the estate. I was shocked how everything had happened so quickly. In my mind, I tied that phone call to this outcome. I felt much pain because of it and I repeat, I wondered what my son would have thought of this situation.

I remembered Janice telling me in the very beginning, when the unthinkable happened, that she would hire an attorney to look out for both of us. Later, after all of the above transpired, she stated in a conversation with my mother that she was forced to do "something." I do not need a law degree to know what that "something" was. I knew the laws of Louisiana, about what would happen when there was no will. If she had sat with me at a table and told me what she wanted, I may not have agreed with it, but I would have respected her wishes. I knew that my opinion wouldn't have counted for much, and I would never have contested the fact that my grandson would be taken care of. More than anything, I would have understood her viewpoint because I know firsthand how a mother would want the best for her son.

What I was confused about, however, was the fact that Janice came to my home on my birthday in June, after the three-way with Mr. Jackson and the benefits office, and talked to me. She actually *moved* in with her belongings, perhaps because she knew the house would belong to my grandson and she wanted to send a message—that she was claiming it. Anyway, during my birthday celebration, which she attended with her aunt, she told me she'd work with me. She gave me assurances and made unlikely promises—but all the while things were happening behind my back, and talks were being conducted with attorneys in Shreveport about the estate. Everyone was fully aware of the implications of having no will, and everyone thought it best to leave me in the dark.

I would not have felt so hurt if everyone were honest about their expectations rather than sneaking around behind my back in a parody of what some people call, in various neigborhoods in New Orleans "cutthroat" (and by this I refer to not the city itself—a beautiful city which has faced many challenges and tragedy—but to certain, undesirable elements, namely bad, "no good dirty" individuals, that reside within an urban area. Although I have never used this term myself, I've heard a few people say it from time to time). I would have liked to be asked outright whatever they wanted to know rather than see everyone go around the mulberry bush to find out if I was willed anything or who the beneficiary was while I was in mourning for my son. This was the lowest point of my life, and I was not thinking about the things my son had or didn't have. The same thought would have applied to Janice. I wish that we—Janice and I especially—could have sat down and discussed things face-to-face, honestly and professionally. I'm sure things would have gone differently if we had. I would not have wasted resources and time going to an attorney, and if I was satisfied that my grandson was being cared for, I would have walked away. Things didn't quite happen this way.

Sometime later, I was asked to provide pictures and tapes for a tribute ceremony that I was never invited to. That was a low blow. I have no idea how or for what purpose the tapes or pictures were used. I was completely left out of the process.

Furthermore, no time was wasted when it came to collecting Marquise's assets. Perhaps, as it was known how much I was grieving, it was considered suitable for others to make their move when they did. Everything was taken away so fast I hardly saw it coming. I did hold on to my son's pictures and some other memories, but not without a fight. Another thing that happened soon after Marquise's death was that Janice came to visit to collect my son's Escalade, which was parked just outside my house.

"It has nails in the tires," she told me and proceeded to take the car.

Later, she stated to my mother that she was "forced" to act a certain way. My mother asked her why she hadn't talked to me about it, and the response was, "I wanted to protect my son." I say, protect him from whom? From his loving grandmother? That was some kind of statement, and it shocked me, although perhaps, I pondered, she may have spoken out of grief or didn't mean it quite that way. Nonetheless, those words were said and we never got a chance to iron this out.

Needless to say, I was surprised beyond belief when my son was mentioned by the media as having a "fiancée" when he died—especially because there had not been no engagement to speak of. Well, to be true, there was one right after the Super Bowl in Jacksonville; but it was later canceled. As I have already explained, the only thing that linked her to my son after that was the baby. During the year before he died, Marquise was living the life of a single person. He knew he had heavy responsibilities towards his son; and in many ways, that included taking care of the mother, but that was all there was to it.

Then, I learned that Darrell Jackson was assisting in some capacity with respect to the administration of my son's estate, as if to protect and promote her interests, and my confusion grew. It has even been reported in some print and Web articles that Marquise's teammates have provided financial help to my grandson and his mother. This, I do not begrudge in the least, as long as Marquise's son gets to benefit the most from these blessings.

Janice is now in possession of (that is, using) two cars that belonged to Marquise: a BMW and a large SUV. Two other cars are presently in Boston, while two others are parked in front of Marquise's house. Or rather, the cars are all tied up in the estate, still pending a decision of the court, but only two are parked at the big house that Marquise had bought for himself. My son's three story condo and the home he purchased for me are also in probate.

Janice told me that she has not decided what to do with the cars yet. I cannot help but question, What one person needs six cars? And if so, who would use so many cars? This, I imagine, is a relative thing, subject to pure speculation. Perhaps they will be used to pay off debt. As far as I'm concerned, I have no idea. I am an outsider to this process.

In the list of cars under probate, I include the 1967 Lincoln which was supposed to go to Marquise's grandmother. It was still in my son's name when he passed away (he was working on it, fixing it for his Big Ma) so that was gone too. If Marquise were found alive today and learned all of this, I try to imagine what he'd say to it.

Another thing I think about is, who will be enjoying the cars in the future? Will my grandson benefit a little from this? These things should be all for the little one, but as we all know, car values depreciate and in fourteen years, when my grandson is fit to drive, all these vehicles will probably have become something akin to scrap metal.

I grasp the importance of this and deeply desire that Marquise's offspring be taken care of. I know that I would have done all in my power to make sure he would be, and today it is Janice's sole job to do so. He is now all I have left and I wish I could see more of him. I miss him terribly, sometimes more than others.

However, depriving a grieving mother of all she holds dear is despicable, to say the least. Everything that was given to me prior to my son's death and grandson's birth, including personal mementos that are very valuable to me, are being taken away from me, added to my son's estate, which is in probate.

I was told that Marquise had a lot of debt, but I have no idea to what extent this is so because I have no right to look at his records. As Mr. Jackson summarily put it, "Leave Ms. Sherry out of it."

One day, I was speaking to Janice about this, trying to make sense of the mess; and she told me, "Ms. Sherry, haven't you received enough?" I responded that no, it wasn't, not after twenty-five years of hard work together, my son and I. Her question came out sounding like an implication that I was hungry for money, whereas all I wanted was to keep what Marquise had given me before he passed. I bit my tongue after that and remembered that it was not just about me. Still, as I always do, I wondered what Marquise would have thought of that remark.

Certain things are clearly not to be. The house Marquise built for me was mortgaged to the hilt, and I could not meet the expense of maintaining or finishing it. I was told I could live in it, but there was no doubt that I'd not be in a position to make the payments on a $400,000 house. Again, as there was no will and I had no access to my son's papers, I was forced to let it go. It pains me mostly because it was my son's gift to me, and I couldn't keep it. Today, I have moved to more modest lodgings, which I can more easily afford with a government paycheck.

This is not a question of illegal appropriation, but it is a matter of doing what's right. Where money is concerned, bad blood is always a factor. I recognize that people who have struggled all their lives may want to grasp such an opportunity at wealth, and I appreciate the importance of making sure that my only grandson will have a comfortable life. What I don't understand is, why would anyone want to take my memories away? Why would anyone want to deprive me of the bits and pieces belonging to my son that are all I have left of him today? This is all I want—they can keep the rest. But in these matters, there are no bounds and reason is often not a factor.

That said, I wish to remark that it is abhorrent to use a person's death for one's personal gain, and I hope that this is not what is happening in my family's case. Aside of those close to me who have loved and cared for Marquise all of his life, there will always be people who are more interested in the things he left behind. This is so despite the fact that Marquise's loved ones may be left to struggle in the interim. I wish to say that nothing is more pure and beautiful than love and the truth, and what goes around always comes around.

I was once more faced with the true state of affairs recently, during this year's Super Bowl game. A few days before the game, I received a call from Mr. Kraft who asked me if I was attending the Super Bowl. Word had come to him that I had received no invitation. Mr. Kraft was quite surprised to learn that—I'm sure he thought that someone would have arranged for my attending the game.

But what Mr. Kraft didn't know was that when Mr. Jackson was talking to me on the phone one day, I asked him why my family hadn't been contacted about the tickets. I did not know what had happened to the tickets which were supposed to go to me and my mother. He told me that when he asked the Patriots administration and game organizers about inviting me to the game, they told him they thought "it would not be a good idea" for me to go. He told me that he had to purchase his own tickets.

Furthermore, Janice also called and stated that she was having problems getting her ticket, that she was going to get a ticket from a friend; so since my mother had decided she was not going, I was thinking of holding that extra ticket for her if I had been invited. I later discovered that four tickets had been reserved for Janice. I never saw one of them. I felt undermined, because I would have been happy to purchase the tickets. I was not expecting them to be free. Why had Marquise's family been left out? Why was I not told about those four tickets? I received lie after lie, and when one tells a lie, it must be supported by more lies. Many questions remained unanswered.

After talking to Mr. Kraft, I called my brother in Alabama because I knew he'd have wanted to come, but it was too short notice to make flight arrangements. He said he'd try to meet me out there, but he never made it. I'm aware, however, that Mr. Kraft did what he could and got me a seat at the game. Within days of talking to him, I would be flown to Arizona on an all-expenses-paid trip.

When Janice found out that I was coming to the game, she called me the day before to tell me that she might not attend. Then, before I left, Mr. Jackson called to ask me whether "I was sure I wanted to go to the game." I thought to myself, *What kind of question is that? The team had been wearing my son's decal all year and he was asking me if I wanted to watch them play the final game with the "91" on their helmets?* I'm from the old school and this incident reminded me of one thing my parents used to say, "When you tell one lie, you must be ready to say another one to back it up." I also listened to my grandparents say many times, "You will have to go bed late at night and wake up early in the morning to fool me."

Despite the setbacks, I enjoyed seeing Arizona; it was the first time for me visiting this state. Happy to have had the opportunity to experience it, I immersed myself in the scenery of the mountains, cactuses and stuccoed homes. The latter reminded me of Marquise's house.

When I arrived at the hotel, I found out that all the players' parents were staying there. The arrangements would have been the same as those made the last time when my family attended the Super Bowl championship game in Jacksonville, Florida. However, circumstances obviously made things different this time. I never expected Mr. Kraft to have to do this for me, but he did. I remember how great he had been when Marquise died—he had flown the entire organization and all team members over for the funeral and paid all the funeral expenses. At this point, I expected Mr. Jackson to look out for me as Marquise's mother. I felt in my heart that he should have had the same care for me as he had for my grandson's mother because my son, who trusted him, was gone. I was wrong.

Before the game, Mr. Jackson suggested helping me find my seat. After I found out where I was seated, I asked him where all the others would be sitting. He showed me where by pointing at the area and I could not crush the sharp pang of pain that lanced through me. I am very grateful for Mr. Kraft's invitation; but going there, and watching Darrell and his friends sitting in the seats reserved for family—from my nondescript seating up high practically in the nosebleed section—was too much to bear. Darrell had told me that they'd purchased the tickets, but my question was, How were all these people sitting next to each other—and in the seats reserved for family—if they had in actual fact bought these tickets randomly? Do they *sell* those specific seats at these kind of events? As I mentioned before, and I repeat, they were all seated in the "family" section, the area where all the players' parents usually sit together (I wondered, *Four people in this group, the same number of tickets that had been reserved for Marquise's family . . . What would my son think?*).

I decided immediately that it would be best to return to my hotel and watch the game in my room because I am near sighted and I'd have a better view by watching the screen. So seeing how distraught I was, Janice promised me that they would bring me down to sit next to them, and they did.

When I joined them, I observed that the party looked happy, like they had cause to celebrate. Of course, who wouldn't, in their position? Those seats may have been meant for my family—so the thought sprung in my mind about what else Mr. Jackson and his party could be enjoying that once belonged to my son. My mind started spinning. If you were in my situation, what would you think?

As soon as I sat down I felt tears brimming in my eyes—the emotion was too strong. A heart-wrenching picture was there, right before my very eyes. I know that Marquise would have hated this. The pain has been locked inside me so long, and I've kept quiet, trying to be brave and holding back from opening my heart. Whatever is inside me now, I must share with you. Whatever I see, I must tell you. Whatever I hear and learn, I must write about—my happiness, my pain, my disappointments. Mostly, there was the feeling of being lost and shut off from the rest of the world. But behind every façade, there is an undeniable truth. And that truth shines through despite our desperate attempts to hide it.

I hate to admit this, but I felt like an afterthought. If Mr. Kraft hadn't sent me the ticket, nobody would have thought about inviting me to this place where my son's star should have been shining. One thing that came out of this experience is that I managed to tell Janice just how I felt. I had no intention of talking about it, but she asked me a direct question. So I went straight out and told her that I was upset.

I remember having asked Mr. Jackson one question a while back when he came to visit me on my job: Where did the fiancée idea come from? How is everyone claiming that Marquise was engaged when in the family we were told, by Marquise, that he wasn't? He claimed he did not know where that came from.

Despite all the confusion and drama, I was expecting some sort of closure—a finale—in memory of Marquise from the event's organizers, as this would have been the first Super Bowl after his death. He would have been proud to be on the team with a perfect record right until the end when the Giants took the final prize. Despite this final loss, it would have been an incredible journey, I'm sure. The Patriots' helmets bore Marquise's 91 number in silent, subtle remembrance (as I have already stated, they had worn the decal throughout the season in honor of my son). I also met some wonderful people who spoke to me warmly about Marquise, and told me how they thought he was special because of what he did. In this sense, the good certainly outweighed the bad of this experience.

I do want to apologize to my son's fans who were expecting a lot more in tribute to Marquise. I received countless phone calls and e-mails to this effect—all day and all night before and after the event. They were disappointed about the turn of events, but as far as I'm concerned, I'm simply grateful.

As I sat with the others throughout the game and observed their interactions, I could see that theirs was a well-organized party, and I honestly felt like an intruder, like I didn't belong there. There was something wrong with that. Mr. Jackson knew that I had my ticket because he'd read about it in the Boston Globe. He claimed that in his group everyone had bought their own ticket, but I found that hard to believe, considering where they were sitting.

That's when it really hit me: "Your son isn't here any more. That's why you're being treated this way."

I wanted to go back to my hotel room and pour my grief within those four walls, but I stayed and watched the game. I didn't want to be discourteous to Mr. Kraft, who had done his best to get me there and had been so kind as to arrange my trip in the last minute. In many ways, I wish to thank Mr. Kraft because he allowed me the opportunity to see things in living color. My son sometimes liked to say, "This is a grim world we live in. People don't have a heart." And I hated to think, then and there, that he was right. Somehow, I'm glad he wasn't there to witness all of this—but if he was there, I'm sure none of it would have happened quite that way.

After the game, Janice communicated to me that she was tired and not in the mood for the after party. Everybody else claimed to be just as worn-out.

The idea was to see me safely in my hotel room. That strategy appeared to me to be a very efficient way to get rid of an unwanted companion. Was my impression correct? I do not know with absolute certainty, but instincts are very powerful and I couldn't shake that thought. Ms. Sherry, it was clear, had indeed been "left out."

The next morning, I got my answer when I found out that everyone had, in fact, left the hotel soon after I was driven there and gone straight to the after party. It was clear as glass that my presence was neither wanted nor appreciated.

Seeing what had happened during the game and then letting my mind dwell on what I saw and heard, I felt hurt and disgusted. Saddened, I felt relief that at least I had made it through the game. I was prepared for my return home. I wanted to be surrounded by love again—by my mother and my family. During those few days in Arizona, I felt stifled by the artfulness and lies that hung in the air. I could say that being settled back at home, safe and sound, I felt as if I could win all life's battles.

I do not wish to appear ungrateful to my son's fans, but some things a grieving mother cannot countenance. At this point, I pray that my beloved grandson will truly be taken care of in the end. I pray that his interests are firmly etched in the hearts of those around him. His present and future welfare should be a priority, and the alternative—something equal to those situations where innocent creatures are used as a pawn or tool for someone else's interests—is not something I ever wish to face or instigate. Once more, I wish to stress that I am not accusing anyone of less-than-ethical behavior, but I worry about my grandson nonetheless. I never want to lose him. I never want to see him shed a tear.

I know that Marquise loved me and his family, and it saddens me to see that what would have been his fondest wishes are not being carried out by some people that he trusted. Losing everything in the aftermath is not what I imagined would happen. I thought we would come together in harmony and sort things out. It is so terrible when pain hits you twice—the first time with the loss of your son and the second time with the actions of people who should hold your child's interests and desires at heart.

I never realized how important it is to have something, a piece of paper, that can speak for you when you cannot speak for yourself any longer. All it takes is pen and paper, but it can make such a difference! If you haven't done so yet, write a will! The popular saying goes, *Where there's a will there's a way*. But I also say that *where there's no will there's no way*. Writing a will is a very valuable process, which can give your loved ones piece of mind or, on the other hand, undue pain when things are left unsaid.

XVII

THE KINDNESS OF STRANGERS

When Marquise passed away, an online guest book was created for people to leave their personal messages to our family. I was both surprised and overwhelmed at the feedback we received. It was like a dam had broken, giving way to an unrelenting flood of compassion and sympathy.

These messages did not only come from people my family knew well or was acquainted with in some manner. People I had never met, people Marquise had never met, poured their hearts out and sent us words of comfort. I will never forget these great kindnesses of strangers which filled my heart, if not with joy, with peace and dignity and, once again, pride in my son.

Marquise's work on earth had been considered done, and a Higher Power claimed and embraced him. He had worked hard and helped many, and it was as if God was saying it was time for him to rest.

Too young by half and too full of energy and spirit to go just yet, but who am I to argue with the Almighty? He sees and knows all, and I'm just a little spoke in the wheel.

In the following pages, you'll have the opportunity to read some of those messages from strangers that I mentioned a few paragraphs ago. There were myriad messages, too many to fit into this little book, so I had to choose a few for publication. That is not to say that the others are not as important. It was a hard decision for me to decide which would go here because each and every one of those e-mails means the world to me. My intention was to extract the essence of these letters and select those which would give you a deeper insight into Marquise's mind and disposition.

The letters say that Marquise was kind to others and always had time to extend a helping hand. They say he was an inspiration and a hero to those who aspired to be like him. Even people who had never met him felt his spirit. There can be no greater compliment and honor to one's memory than this.

Through these letters, I want you to recognize these facts about my son, not because he was so unique, but simply because he was human. In this age of technology and impersonal relationships, Marquise had found humanity in all living things. He knew the importance of the wonderful and sometimes rare gifts of family, friends, respect, and laughter. He had also faced injustice, but all of that could not bend his incredible optimism and drive.

This is something I wish all young people would know. If you are a parent, please pass this book on to your sons and daughters. If you are a young man or woman who still needs to find a path in life, hold this as a guide to positive living. Never stop having dreams, and once you have them, never give up on them.

To learn more about Marquise's personal stats and the highlights of his career, please visit Patriots.com. I hope you will enjoy reading the following testimonials as I hope you have enjoyed reading the rest of this book.

NOTE: All names have been removed for privacy protection purposes

Selections From The Guest Book For Marquise Hill

To the family and loved ones of Marquise Hill. I received a story via e-mail once that spoke about the day a person is born and the day they go "home." It stated that what is important is what happens between those dates.

The media said that this young man helped those that suffered during Hurricane Katrina and others that were in need. God looks at your works, not that you sit in church on Sunday. He looks at your works . . . It seems as if Marquise's works were complete, and the Lord can truly say, "A job well done."

You are blessed to have had and learned from the example set by this angel of the Lord.

(Atlanta, GA)

* * *

I first met Marquise two years ago when he was doing volunteer work through the United Way. He was one of four New England Patriots who were building a wheelchair ramp for a poor old woman.

Marquise was the biggest man out there that day in terms of physical size and in terms of heart. He pitched right in and did more than his share of the labor that needed to get done, and he did it with a smile! After the work was done, he took the time to go inside of the house and visit with the lady just to show that he cared.

He and I talked a few times over the telephone after that day and became friends. Mainly he sought my counsel about finance and how he might be able to set aside money for the benefit of his family. Also because as a former army colonel, I have counseled dozens of young men just like him.

Marquise was a man with a big heart who will indeed be missed.

(Baintree, MA)

* * *

That man is a success who has lived well, laughed often, and loved much. Who has gained the respect of intelligent men and the love of children. Who has filled his niche and accomplished his task. Who leaves the world better than he found it . . . Who never lacked appreciation of earth's beauty or failed to express it. Who looked for the best in others and gave the best he had. My sincerest condolences to the family.

(MA)

* * *

Marquise, you are the perfect example of a man who has succeeded! Rest in peace.

(Stratham, NH)

* * *

To the Hill family:

I met and worked with Marquise in the summer of 2003. At the time, my son was eleven years old; he was beginning to play basketball. One day, my son came to work with me; there he met Marquise. He was in awe of this gentle giant.

A few days later, Marquise presented me with a football, signed by the entire 2003 LSU team, as a gift and inspiration to my son. My son is now fifteen, a dedicated athlete in his own right. We have talked about Marquise for days now. His goodness and grace will indelibly be etched in the hearts of a young man and his mom.

(Baton Rouge, LA)

* * *

To the Hill family, I am sorry for your loss, my heart goes out to you. I am a big Patriots fan and had the pleasure of meeting Marquise two years ago at Foxborough Stadium. Marquise made me laugh and touched my heart; I will never forget your son. He was and will always be a wonderful man in my eyes. And I will forever hold Marquise in my heart, his number 1 fan from Bermuda.

(Southampton, Bermuda)

* * *

Sherry, as your former school principal at Our Lady Star of the Sea Catholic School, you and your family have my deepest sympathy for the loss of your wonderful son. May the Lord give you peace during this period of bereavement.

(Slidell, LA)

* * *

Mrs. Sherry, I've spoke to you on many occasions while getting in touch with Marquise. My heart and prayer go out to you and the entire family. Marquise was not only a friend, but he was an inspiration to me to get in the sports management field. While at DeLaSalle, I watched your son grow up right in front of my eyes. Your son was not only a great person, but he was a leader. This is not just a loss for everyone, but its Marquise calling from the man upstairs. Mrs. Sherry, we all feel this pain, but God will always be looking over us. Only now, he has Marquise looking with him. Mrs. Sherry, I would love to help any way possible. I would love to put on an event remembering my good friend and your great son. Thank you and God bless.

(New Orleans, LA)

* * *

"He Himself has said, I will not in any way fail you nor give you up nor leave you without support" (Hebrews 13:5).

Ms. Sherry and family,

May God's presence ease your trembling spirit and give you rest. He knows how you feel. He is aware of your circumstances and ready to be your strength, your grace, and your peace. Marquise was definitely a loving and kindhearted young man. He definitely made my nephews', Justin and Jarrett, eyes glistened with awe.

When what you are feeling is simply too deep for words, and nothing anyone does or says can provide you with the relief you need, God understands. Cast all of your cares on Him . . . and believe.

(Baton Rouge, LA)

* * *

Mrs. Hill, Marquise was your baby, but remember he also is God's baby; that's why God called him home to be with him. Just keep your hand in God's hand and stay strong, and one day you'll see him again.

(New Orleans, LA)

* * *

Yet we, the people, mourn; but *our God* is rejoicing that this great man has joined him in *heaven.* To the Hill family, be not dismayed whatever betides you, for God will take care of you! Look to the hills from whence cometh your help, for it all comes from the Lord.

You'll be missed down here on earth, but heaven is shouting for this great victory!

(Lakeland, FL)

* * *

RIP, Marquise. You may be gone, but definitely not forgotten. I only knew you for a brief time as a coworker at Jazzland, but knew when I saw you that you would be something special. Though our time was brief, I never forgot your name; and whenever I saw you play and live your dreams, my eyes glowed because you were my friend and associate. I was extremely proud when I saw you lead LSU to the national championship, and even though I wasn't a big fan of the New England Patriots, I was proud to see you win the Super Bowl . . . You accomplished your dreams and made a difference. I thank you for coming into my life and promise that you will never leave . . . with much love, you will always be missed, Marquise.

Love,
(Jazzland c/o 2000)
(New Orleans, LA)

* * *

May God's love and mercy help your family through this terrible ordeal. Marquise was really a soldier in God's army for all the many blessings he shared with others just being in his presence, watching him always give

110 percent in everything he did from the classroom, to the football field, to the giving of himself in the rebuilding aftermath of New Orleans, to his own life to "put someone else first!" Let this gifted young black man's legacy be not in vain, but let him teach us how to stand strong despite the inevitable! Marquise Hill, take a bow because you are another one of God's servant that he has told, "Well done!"

(New Orleans, LA)

* * *

What a class guy Marquise was! You can truly be proud of your son and the way he represented your family, LSU, and the Patriots on and off the field. May his eternal soul rest in the peace of your loving God! Hold strong to your wonderful memories of your beloved son, father, and fiancé. God will give you the courage and strength to see each new day. You will see Marquise again!

(Marrero, LA)

* * *

From the day your uncle James Hill introduced me to you, I knew that you would be forever embedded into my memories. I will always remember you "lil brother" for the smiles you gave me—"94" FOREVER AND A DAY!

(New Orleans, LA)

* * *

To my dearest cousin, Sherry, and family: We are remembering you and honoring your most beloved and beautiful son, Marquise. It deeply saddens our hearts as we share with you in grief during this time of sorrow. We send you thoughts of peace and comfort with love. May all the loving memories of Marquise sustain you, keep you, and bless you.

(Katona, NY)

* * *

May your hearts soon be filled with wonderful memories of joyful times together with Marquise as you celebrate a life well lived.

(New Orleans, LA)

* * *

Dear Sherry:

After reading all of the wonderful thoughts and prayers for your son, I realize what a special person he was. Even though I didn't know him personally, I can tell how deeply and positively he impacted so many people's lives. His death will not be in vain.

My deepest sympathy to you and your family,

(New Orleans)

* * *

Sherry,

I have known you for a while, and I remember you spoke highly on how proud you were as a mom to your son. I enjoyed hearing you talking about him and his accomplishment and his becoming a successful young man. You have my deepest sympathy on the loss of your son. He'll still always be in your heart and still be around you. You're in my prayers.

(River Ridge, LA)

* * *

Sherry, my prayers are with you in this time of sorrow. I remember when you came to a toastmaster's meeting, all excited that Marquise was going to the Super Bowl! What a proud momma you were that day, and a proud momma you should still be, for the magnificent son you raised.

I send you also my love.

(Chalmette, LA)

* * *

My thoughts and prayers are with this young player who had the chance of being the next Ty Warren and all-around great player. I hope the Pats honor you and wear your number on their uniforms.

RIP, Marquise Hill

(Mexico, ME)

* * *

His memory will live on forever,
Remember Marquise for who he truly
was and not how he left this world,
My prayers to his family.

(Jacksonville, FL)

* * *

I am so sorry to hear of your loss. May your hearts soon be filled with wonderful memories of joyful times together, and may the love of friends and family carry you through your grief. May God bless you and your family in this time of sorrow.

(Culpepper, VA)

* * *

The times in life that are the hardest to have faith is when we must have the most faith. Marquise Hill was a wonderful person, loved by all and would be missed greatly. I find comfort in the Bible—John 3:16 and 1 Peter 5:6-7 . . . God bless.

(Baton Rouge, LA)

* * *

The Hill family, losing a son can only be felt by another mother that has gone through the same experience. For me, I can only say that for my mother, it was very painful. I can only say, “God bless,” and that is where she got her strength. Take comfort in all of the responses you get. Your son has touched a lot of people, and that is the best gift of all. In the short time he was here, he probably touched more people than someone that have been here for seventy years. Take comfort in that, and know you raised a respectable son. God is with you. Stay strong. He was loved by millions.

(Oakdale, CT)

* * *

Dear Hill family,

Marquise was a real man; he helped those who needed help and died the same way, regardless of its outcome for him. As a lifelong Patriots fan, I too am in mourning for we lost a star on the rise. In his last effort to save his friend, he showed that, no matter what, he was a star on the rise! God bless, and may peace be with you. We will all miss Marquise, both as a player and as a man. Remember God takes those he wants for special deeds when he wants. We have no control over our fate.

Marquise did nothing but good with his time here on earth; God must have something great planned for him in heaven!

(Florham Park, NJ)

* * *

To the family of Mr. Hill, I was saddened to hear of the loss of your loved one. My sons played football for college, and I often had a fear that something would happen to them because the game was very rough, but they came through all right. You never can imagine that something like this would happen, but if I may leave you with something from the Bible in Revelation 21:4, God said he will wipe out every tear from their eyes, and death will be no more; neither pain nor outcries be anymore, the former things has passed away. So you see, Jehovah has given his son the authority to resurrect the dead, and soon we can see our dead loved one again. So stay in prayer and remember that God love us all, and he wants us to put all our burden on him, and he will give us rest. I hope these words brought some comfort to you and your family.

(Dover, DE)

* * *

I was able to have the pleasure of meeting Marquise during his first year with the Patriots. I must say, Ms. Sherry, you raised a fine young man who spoke very highly of you and his entire family. I know at this time you and the rest of the Hill family is going through a great loss, and my prayers are with you. I'm still in great disbelief over his death, and I will miss Marquise dearly. Again, you have my deepest sympathy and prayers.

(Boston, MA)

* * *

There are greater measures of a person than success in business and sports, but Marquise was young, and his better days were still ahead of him. I'm sad that I never got to know Marquise's kind nature and generosity while he was a player; everything that I read about him now makes it crystal clear why the Patriots valued him as a teammate. My prayers go out to the Hill family. Marquise was a fine young man.

(Duxbury, MA)

Letter from a Mother to WWLTV

On the next page, you will find a letter that was written by a mother who had been touched by Marquise through one of his many acts of kindness. Neither Marquise nor I had been acquainted with this lady, but Marquise had nonetheless made a positive impact in her son's life. This is just one of many stories where Marquise had shown his mettle—that of a heart at least as big as his body.

This letter, when the TV station forwarded it to me, moved me so much that I couldn't hold back tears of pride and loss. I read it and grieved for my son all over again.

Because he wouldn't be able to do what he did for that boy anymore.

Because I wouldn't be able to see his smile anymore. Only in my memory.

Lord, please grant him eternal peace.

Letter from a mother to WWLTV

The following e-mail was sent to WWL-TV on May 30, two days after the body of Marquise Hill was found in Lake Pontchartrain. I was also mailed a copy of it (some names have been omitted for copyright purposes or to protect the privacy of the persons involved. The full letter, including names, may be found at the WWLTV website under the heading "Mother says Marquise Hill made a difference in her son's life"):

June 1, 2007
To whom it concerns:
My name is XXXXX, I reside in Boston, Massachusetts.

Marquise Hill was definitely awesome and my son and I were able to experience this first hand.

When my son XXXXX was 15-years-old, he was a very large guy. 6'4" tall and weighs 275 pounds with a size 15 shoe. I was desperately looking for a mentor for him to help appreciate and accept his size, as well as excelling in a sport that he loved: football.

I wrote a letter to the Patriot fan mail page and directed it to two of the larger players on the team whom I thought would be helpful, one of them Marquise Hill. He responded through his agent, XXXXXX.

Marquise apologized for responding so late to my email and asked what he could do for my son. I asked him if he knew of any mentoring type of programs that would be good for a boy of my son's size. Marquise went on to ask me if it was hard finding my sons clothes or shoes, and I told him that shoes were difficult to find because he wore a size 15.

But Marquise told me to meet him at Foot Action on Newbury Street so he could buy my son some shoes. It was great! Especially being a working mother of four; and raising a son in particular is a struggle. We searched the store for this hard to find size 15, but we finally found a pair and my son's face was ecstatic! Not only because we found a pair in his size, but because someone actually took time out of their day to meet with him; someone who initially met us by answering a call for help.

We exchanged phone numbers and my son chatted with him periodically until the tragic Katrina floods. We lost contact with Marquise because his cell phone number was New Orleans based, but we prayed that his family was safe, along with all the others.

Marquise Hill gave my son the best advice as he drove us to our car that afternoon and said, "The first thing I did when I signed my contract was buy my momma a house . . . Make sure you take care of your mama, I love my mama and would do anything for her and that is more important than anything!"

The other night, when I saw the news that they recovered Marquise's body, I cried all night and still have a lump in my throat. To think someone so special was taken away; so young, so full of life and generosity. But I'm glad my son was able to meet such a positive person.

My son is now 17-years-old and he's grown considerably (6'7" and 350 pounds). He plans on attending football camp this summer and hopes to be able to one day pass on the lessons he learned on that day when he met Marquise Hill. Marquise was a true hero, respectful, proud, caring, and a gentle giant! Please, if you are able to pass this on to his family it would be greatly appreciated!

Best Regards . . .

The Marquise Hill Foundation

Marquise and I had often talked about creating a foundation to help others in need. This foundation would focus mostly on helping children achieve their dreams through educational aid, such as contribution of charitable funds to high school and grade school athletic programs. The foundation would also seek to assist St. Jude Hospital in Memphis, Tennessee, provide single parent support, aid Katrina victims (particularly the elderly and the ill), and work with troubled youth through the creation of a monitoring program and the establishment of the Marquise Hill Scholarship Fund for high school students.

After his passing, I decided to proceed with our plans and set up the Marquise Hill Foundation as we had agreed. I am proud to continue his legacy and my intent is that though this non-profit organization, my son's memory will continue to provide renewed hope in the lives of many people. You may forward your taxable contributions to the address below:

Contact address:
The Marquise Hill Foundation
P. O. Box 852
Slidell, LA 70459-0852

"Hey Ma"

To hear you say "Hey Ma" would be music to my ears
To hear you say "Hey Ma" from you, son, would dry up all my tears
Taking care of my heart for the rest of my years
I would give all I have and know it would be worth it
Just to hear you say "Hey Ma" once again

Thank you, son, for all the happiness and joy you brought me over the years
The smiles, the rewards
The love of mother and son
You showed me in words, you showed me in deeds
You showed me with the beautiful home, cars, limo rides, and rings and all of the dreams you strove to make real
But all these things I'd give up in a heartbeat—just to hear you say "Hey Ma" once again

This home, these rooms still echo your sweet words
"Hey Ma, hey Ma!"
You'd always say to make me turn and look your way
I still feel your strength
The hard work, the pain, the obstacles thrown in your way
Together you and I
Jumping life's hurdles day after day
But all of these memories I'd give up in a heartbeat—just to hear you say "Hey Ma" once again

You rolled through your career collecting six championship rings
A Super Bowl ring was yours too in the end
A gentle giant they called you, with love and devotion
But all of this glory, all of this fame, I'd have you give up in a heartbeat—just to hear you say "Hey Ma" once again!

Love live inside you, son, forever and a day

A Mother's Prayer

Son, you left without a notice, a thought, or a plan
No will to speak of, no message with paper and ink
The law gives instructions, provisions, and such
But regardless, your wishes should have mattered without so much as a blink
Your heart would be broken because you trusted mankind
Because you're gone, and no one paid you mind

I know you loved me, your family, your son
A good man you grew, like a good father you cherished
Looking out for our future with devotion and care

No pain, no suffering could replace your loving gaze
For that alone I'd give the rest of my days
I pray that your name won't be sullied in vain
I pray that your departure won't be used for someone's personal gain
I pray that your loss would cause pain borne only of love
—not merely of greed
Of exploitation, money, and conceit
Of manipulation and deceit
The vultures are buzzing all around, my son . . .
And if that's true, then it's truly a shame
I will let the Lord handle it
In Jesus' name

Marquise last photo taken by a friend near the lake in 2006 while we were still dislocated in Baton Rouge after Katrina. Thank you, son, for 24 rewarding years. You made me proud. You are truly missed. Your "Hey Ma" for the rest of my life.

This page is for version tracking purposes only. This is not part of the book and will be deleted when the book goes into Author Copy Stage.

Designed by :

Corrections Done by :

Date :